Working in Art and Design

Peter Green

Batsford Academic and Educational Ltd
London

©Peter Green 1983
First published 1983

All rights reserved. No part of this publication
may be reproduced, in any form or by any means,
without permission from the Publisher.

Typeset by Progress Filmsetting
and printed in Great Britain by
The Pitman Press Ltd
Bath
for the publishers
Batsford Academic and Educational Ltd
an imprint of B T Batsford Ltd
4 Fitzhardinge Street
London W1H 0AH

British Library Cataloguing in Publication Data
Green, Peter
Working in art and design.
11. Art—Vocational guidance—Great Britain
I. Title
702'.3'4111   N8350

ISBN 0 7134 253 3

Contents

Acknowledgment 7
Captions to photographs between pages 96 and 97

1 The artist, designer and craftsperson in society 9
   1 The artist and designer 9
   2 What is Art and Design and are they different? 11
   3 The crafts today 13
      Where does the craftsman fit in?—
      The crafts revival 15
   4 How do artists, designers and craftsman work?—what do they do? 16
   5 The growth of the design profession, professional bodies and the art schools 22

2 Before you go to art school 25
   1 Can anyone be an artist? 25
   2 Is training necessary? 26
   3 What reasons may you have for choosing art? 27
   4 What abilities and skills are needed? 30
   5 From secondary school to art school 33
      (i) Why a foundation course? 33
      (ii) When do I decide? 35
      (iii) The folder of work 37
      (iv) What other preparations can I make before going to college? 39

3 College studies 41
   1 Introduction—the national picture 41
      Degrees and Diplomas 42
      Who validates the courses—CNAA, DATEC, the universities and colleges 43
      Some of the choices to be made 44
   2 The Nature of 'Art School' work 46
      Art history and complementary studies 47
   3 The broad areas of study and specialisation 48
      Fine Art 49

    Graphic Design   49
    Textiles/Fashion   50
    Three-Dimensional Design   51
    Engineering Design   52
4 The courses—their scope and content   52
    Specialist courses   53
    (i)   Foundation studies   53
    (ii)   Specialist CNAA degree courses   54
    (iii)   DATEC diplomas and certificates   57
    (iv)   College diplomas and certificates and professional qualifications   59
    (v)   Engineering design—courses and training   63
    (vi)   Art teaching   64
    (vii) Post-graduate study—advanced studies   67
    (viii) Part-time vocational courses   69
           Trade based training   69
    General courses   69
    (ix)   History of art   69
    (x)   Combined multi-disciplinary and general degrees   71
    (xi)   The diploma in higher education (DipHE)   73
5 Entry qualifications—how and when to apply   74
    (i)   Foundation courses   74
    (ii)   BA (Hons) specialist art and design degrees (CNAA)   75
    (iii)   Non-specialist degrees at polytechnics and colleges of higher education   77
    (iv)   University degrees in art and design, including art history   77
    (v)   DATEC diplomas and certificates   78
    (vi)   Art teacher training (including CDT)   79
    (vii) College diplomas and certificates, post-graduate courses in art and design, engineering courses   80
6 Grants   81

4 Working as a designer, craftsman or artist   84
  1 Introduction   84
  2 Where will you work?—two broad categories   87
      (i)   Freelance designer, (ii) Staff designer   87
  3 The Industrial designer   89
      (i)   Employing an agent   91
  4 Artists and designer-craftsmen   92
      (i)   Outlets for work   92
      (ii)   A place to work   93

  (iii) Craftsmen and freelance industrial design 94
  (iv) Exhibiting 94
  (v) Grants 94
 5 Legal and financial advice 95

5 Some specific occupations – a broad guide 96
 1 Graphic Design 96
  (i) Advertising and publicity design – advertising art director 97
  (ii) Art editor – magazine and book publishing 98
  (iii) General illustration – books and magazines 99
  (iv) Technical, scientific, medical illustration 100
  (v) Model making 101
  (vi) The typographer 101
  (vii) Layout artists 102
  (viii) The sign designer 102
  (ix) Packaging design 103
  (x) Work as a photographer 104
  (xi) Film animation 105
  (xii) Film making 106
  (xiii) Television graphics 107
  (xiv) Visual aids for education – educational graphics 108
  (xv) Lettering, calligraphy and bookbinding 108
 2 Three-Dimensional Design 109
  (i) The traditional industrial crafts 109
  (ii) Silverware 110
  (iii) Jewellery 111
  (iv) Glassware 112
  (v) Pottery – ceramics 112
  (vi) Furniture 113
  (vii) Work as an industrial or product designer (engineering) 114
  (viii) Model making and technical draughtsmanship 116
  (ix) Design technicians 116
  (x) The interior designer 116
  (xi) Interior decoration 118
  (xii) Exhibition designer 118
  (xiii) Display designer 119
  (xiv) Theatre design – film and television set designer 119
 3 Textiles/Fashion Design 121
  (i) Fashion designer 122
  (ii) Millinery 124
  (iii) Shoes 124

    (iv)   Embroidery   125
    (v)   Lingerie and corsetry   125
    (vi)   Fashion accessories   126
    (vii)   Mens wear—sportswear   126
    (viii)   Associated occupations—
        Technicians, Fashion illustrator, Fashion journalism, Fashion buyer, Paper pattern design   127
    (vix)   Theatrical costume design   128
    (x)   Woven fabrics   129
    (xi)   Knitwear   130
    (xii)   Lace   131
    (xiii)   Printed textiles   132
    (xiv)   Wall paper design   132
    (xv)   Carpets   133
    (xvi)   Plastics, decorative surfaces, floor coverings   133
4   Fine Art   134
    (i)   Art and design historian   134
    (ii)   Museum and gallery curatorship—exhibition and museum assistants   135
    (iii)   Picture restoration—preservation, conservation—the paper conservator   135
    (iv)   Picture research—picture and slide librarian   136
    (v)   The community arts—arts administration   136
    (vi)   Work as a painter, sculptor, printmaker   137
5   Art and Design Teaching   138
    (i)   Primary teaching   138
    (ii)   Secondary schools   139
    (iii)   Further and higher education   139
    (iv)   Art teaching in other institutions   140
    Museums and galleries; Local arts centres; Community Arts projects; Arts administration; Recreational evening classes; Prison service; Art therapy
Notes on Bibliography and Addresses 141
Bibliography and Addresses 142
   1 Journals and periodicals 142
   2 Bibliography 143
   3 Addresses 148

Index 156

Acknowledgment

To cover the breadth of material associated with working in Art and Design has inevitably required help and advice from a large number of people.

My thanks therefore to all colleagues in the Faculty of Art and Design at Middlesex Polytechnic for their extensive help. Most professional areas of work are represented in the Faculty and I have been able to draw heavily on the experience of many subject specialists. Colleagues at Middlesex involved in Art and Design careers advice work with schools have also been especially helpful, along with both past and present students. In addition the Polytechnic's Communications Office was extremely helpful in lending me the photographs taken by Trefor Ball.

D F Cheshire, the Faculty Librarian, has been a tireless researcher on my behalf. He has skilfully collected and collated information and given much helpful professional guidance.

Linda Foster has, more than anyone, contributed a great deal of help and valuable advice, based on her extensive experience with young students entering college and starting their careers. More importantly however she kindly undertook the typing of the final manuscript, together with its many corrections. In many senses therefore this book is a joint production.

Finally, as always, Thelma M Nye has, with patient friendship, edited and steered the production through its various stages and I would like to particularly thank her for her hardwork and encouragement.

Peter Green
Faculty of Art and Design
Middlesex Polytechnic
January 1 1983

Captions to illustrations between pages 96 and 97

General view of graphic design studio

Working at a lathe — an industrial design furniture student obtaining practical experience

Scientific illustration — detailed analytical drawing using a stereo-microscope

Technical graphics — general studio

Film animation — shooting an animated sequence on the rostrum camera

Photo/Computer typesetting — operating the keyboard

Weaving — hand loom workshop

Student exploring textiles and three-dimensional form

Foundation student

Silversmithing/Jewellery — repoussé work, incising a surface pattern into silver

Ceramics — repetition throwing on the wheel

Photographs taken by Trefor Ball and reproduced by kind permission of the Communications Office, Middlesex Polytechnic.

1 The artist, designer and craftsperson in society

1 The artist and designer

We still, in the latter part of the twentieth century, probably find it difficult to say what an artist and designer does. There have always been artists, designers and craftsmen; or at least there have always been people who draw pictures, make things and define and determine the shape of things; and others who build and construct, and convey ideas and information. All these everyday activities are about doing and making, and describe the world of art and design. But somehow we still think the artist is probably a strange creative being and the design process a mysterious activity. Artists and designers, so important to our daily lives, have become rather distant, yet we live in a world of made and manufactured things and everything around us has been designed, whether badly or efficiently.

There is no doubt a tendency to think of 'Art and Design' in rather narrow terms—associated only with the work of painters and sculptors. We are puzzled about what artists do—for we never see jobs advertised for them and we possibly confuse 'design' with vague ideas about 'commercial' art. The reasons for this are complex, but in part it is no doubt due to the fact that art and design has become removed from our daily lives—with the idea of the artist as a special person in his studio and the designer a rare professional working in his drawing office.

The scope of art and design has of course broadened and changed dramatically during this century. New technologies and mass production have changed and extended the work of the artist. No longer is he just the painter of pictures or the decorator of manufactured goods or a hand craftsman. With industrialisation and mass communication the artist's role has extended and the whole field of art and design now embraces most aspects of human life and a wide range of skills and specialisations.

We live in a designed and planned world, where everything around us has been designed by someone. All the things we use, all the images we see, our towns, transport systems, homes and clothes are all in varying degrees the work of the artist and designer, as are the films and television we watch and the books and magazines we read.

The nature of our surroundings is therefore totally determined

The artist, designer and craftsperson in society

by the designer—that's what living in a man-made world means. Someone, somewhere has determined the shape of things. But it's not just the look of things, it's the impact on our lives that makes design so important. The colour, shape and feel of things is obviously very important, not just for our pleasure, but for the ideas they convey; but more significantly our surroundings have got to work for us and this is where the role of the designer comes in. It matters if things don't work—it can either be irritating or disastrous. A badly fitting shoe, or chair, can be annoying or serious to our health, but a badly planned town or tower block can be catastrophic.

So we begin to see that in a designed and planned world the artist/designer is not a luxury or fun person but someone whose work critically affects our lives. Not only our human happiness and comfort, but also our safety, health and industrial and commercial survival as a nation.

We start therefore to measure the work of the designer in terms of how efficient he is and how responsible he is in responding to our needs; he is not just the maker of pretty things or attractive pictures. Not only is the field extremely wide but along with this breadth is the emerging social importance of design as an activity. When we consider how much of our world, in fact all man-made things, are in part the work of the designer then it would seem that there could not be a sufficient number of artists and designers available to do the work.

On the one hand we have this apparent unlimited field for artists and designers to work in, and on the other the incontrovertible fact that many highly trained artists and designers can be under employed. One explanation of this paradox is that so much of the production and manufacturing of goods is undertaken by people with no design training. Which may be one reason why so much ugliness is to be found in the world and why so many things do not work well for us.

The art world claims that the services of good designers should be sought more often, while industry complains that it cannot afford such luxury and that anyhow artists all too often seem unaware of technical and practical requirements. These are traditional arguments which have gone on for years. However, we cannot afford to ignore the vital importance of design if we are to remain competitive as an industrial nation and if the quality of our daily lives is to be improved. Efforts to improve our awareness of the importance of design, have no doubt increased in recent years, and our systems of design education are admired by many other countries. Nevertheless, although many improvements have been made, we still under-use our designers and the nation's visual

The artist, designer and craftsperson in society

standards remain depressingly low.

Gradually things are improving, helped by the growth of design education, and the work of organisations such as the Design Council and Crafts Council. Industries are also realising the value of high design standards—though the current period of economic stringency is bound to be frustrating to designers. However important design is to the health of the nation; recognition of the designer's status in industry continues to be a struggle, and young designers must realise this, however attractive and personally rewarding the life style and work may appear as a student.

2 What is Art and Design and are they different?

Endeavouring to explain or define Art, or what we may mean by Design, is clearly a complicated and almost philosophical debate, outside the scope of this book. However, we do need to be able to make some broad distinction and try to understand with what both activities may be concerned.

Art and design clearly plays an essential part in all our lives, but outside the professional world of artists and designers little is perhaps known about what they do and how they effect our lives. In fact we may argue that art and design is nothing to do with us.

Yet of course we do from time to time visit art galleries and museums and hopefully enjoy looking at pictures, and we certainly look at buildings, watch films and television and go to the theatre, in fact we participate in art and benefit from the work of artists by simply looking and watching.

We also, everyday, make decisions and come in contact with the designer's work when we shop, by thinking about the value, function and purpose of designed things in relation to their style and appearance.

Art and design is therefore all around us and both activities are in a sense indivisible. Artists when painting a picture use colour and design and organise shapes and forms in a 'designerly' way—they in fact 'design' a picture. While designers similarly need to manipulate form, colour and shape and express ideas; so both activities overlap.

Art and design certainly used to be thought of as branches of the same thing, but throughout this century have come to be seen as different activities which nevertheless employ similar skills—and for this reason no doubt are always taught in the same institutions—colleges and schools of art and design.

In actual fact the separate profession of the designer, as we shall see later in this section, is something which has only grown up in the last 60 years or so.

11

The artist, designer and craftsperson in society

Both artists and designers solve problems. However, the so-called 'fine artist' (usually a painter, sculptor or printmaker) solves his own personal problems and sets out to communicate, or express, his own ideas. The designer on the other hand is responsible for solving someone else's problems. He identifies an external need, what someone else needs, and applies his skills to solving that problem.

Design can be described as a social activity concerned with manufacturing and industrial production. It is also invariably a group activity, involving work with other skilled professionals. Fine art on the other hand is a more personal, private and inward-looking individual activity.

Designers of course often paint pictures and painters may, during their careers, be asked to work with designers or are commissioned to design things—the training and specific professional disciplines are different but both are concerned with the world of visual ideas. It is often argued that fine art as a discipline underlies all work and study in art and design, and certainly the skills of drawing and the ability to develop and express ideas visually are fundamental to all design work.

Designers however are concerned with planning and shaping almost every element of our environment, all the commodities we use and all the means and forms by which we communicate. Basically they are concerned with 'made things', articles and utensils for use—things which have got to work. They must determine how these things look and operate and have the responsibility of making them more efficient, more economic, and more attractive. Above all designers must meet the needs of consumers and clients and achieve their ends within strict commercial limits and the constraints of technology and production.

By comparison, painters and sculptors can work in a much freer framework, not necessarily easier, but certainly different. Artists working on their own, exploring their personal ideas and views of the world, can open our eyes to new experience—they can in fact help us see and understand the world. They open up the world of ideas and human reactions and share with us the discoveries of the work of their vision and imagination. As opposed to designers concerned with solving what could be called 'public' problems fine artists operate mainly within the confines of their own 'private' creativity. Their work in a narrow utilitarian sense can be 'useless' in strictly practical terms but it can challenge, excite, delight or make us see things afresh and it must always be an essential part of any civilised society. In fact in a world dominated by mass production, and the threat of mass automation, the world

The artist, designer and craftsperson in society

of the poet, visionary and individual artist has never been so important in balancing the impact of impersonal technology and repetitive conformity.

So artists and designers complement each other—one sets out to work with technology and industry, bringing shape and order to production, while the other maintains and upholds the role of the expressive individual, so essential in a technological world.

3 The crafts today—where does the craftsman fit in—the crafts revival

Strictly speaking designers don't make things. In an industrial society the machine and industry produces and manufactures. The designer draws up the plan—his is the world of the drawing board and prototype (the model for production). But once something is designed and the drawings finished, and prototypes tested, then it's the machine that does the making—that's what mass production and an industrial society is about, hence the phrase 'industrial designer'—someone who designs for industry.

The craftsman, however, historically makes by hand. In a pre-industrial society craftsmen and workmen made everything by hand, gradually developing tools and machines to help ease drudgery and speed up production in response to demand. Before the nineteenth century the designer and craftsman were normally one. The person who had the idea also made the product. The craftsman not only decided on the shape of things, its size, colour and form, but he also made it himself, whether it was a chair, shoe, or cup and saucer.

Today in our complicated industrial society we have divided and separated these activities and almost lost the hand craftsman. Designers tend to work out the idea and then pass it to the machine to make and the craftsman (now referred to as the craftsperson) has been bypassed and, at one stage, looked like disappearing altogether.

Where does the craftsman fit in?

Although their roles may have changed hand-craftsmen and the hand-made object still have their place.

Firstly, even in the world of mass production the craftsperson or model maker has a role. Prototypes and models, or 'one-offs', have to be made for a number of reasons; to see, for example, if a designer's idea works and to show a client, in model form, what a finished product may look like. Designers often work closely with craftsmen model makers who translate their ideas into tangible

The artist, designer and craftsperson in society

production form. Secondly, in the training of designers, hand skills and experience in making is essential. You cannot design for industrial production unless you have experience of how materials behave and what you can do with them. You have to be able to make something yourself before planning for production—so the crafts are necessarily very much a part of the training of designers. More importantly, however, the crafts have had a revival during the second half of this century and still play a very important part in the employment of artists and designers.

Mass production can of course make products widely available and at a price we can all afford and this is one of the primary functions of industry. But mass produced things, by their nature, all look the same. As we have got more used to the machine not everyone wants the same things and a market continues to develop for the individually made 'one-off' object. Many factors have contributed to the revival of crafts; increased affluence, the tourist trade, an interest in our craft heritage (we were once a society of makers), and a desire to own well made things which are different. The revival of the crafts is, in one sense, a very real reaction against mass production.

Many designers and artists therefore also work as craftsmen and the phrase 'designer-craftsman' or 'artist-craftsman' has become a commonplace. What is important is that, like 'art' and 'design'—'craft' and 'design' are also inter-related and can live together.

The designer in his career may both design for industry and design and make things himself. In other words he can work for both markets. Some artists set up workshops and small businesses and sell their own craft-made objects and the recent consumer market boom has obviously helped keep the crafts very much alive.

Others, while working for industry, may also produce hand craft objects for outlets in shops and galleries. A good example of this would be a chair or furniture designer who may both design for mass production (where he doesn't actually make the chair) and in addition, in his own workshop, make a limited number of hand made chairs which he sells himself.

If a designer-craftsman is working only in the hand made field then he obviously cannot produce large quantities, so the emphasis is on originality and craft qualities. While there is a continuing demand for such products they are inevitably more expensive and tend to attract only the top end of the commercial consumer market.

Many people of course cannot afford hand made craft products but may nevertheless be dissatisfied with the conformity of mass

The artist, designer and craftsperson in society

produced goods and look for something a little more personal. This trend has helped encourage a growing middle range market for young designers and craftsmen, and what is beginning to emerge is the setting up of small workshops whose capacity is half way between large mass production and expensive individual craftwork.

To set up machinery and a production line to manufacture objects is very expensive. Industry therefore has to produce large quantities and keep producing for a long time to make expenditure and initial outlay on plant worthwhile. People of course can get tired of such repetition; though it obviously has many advantages, and there is therefore opportunity for small workshops to fill the middle ground between cheap mass production and expensive hand craft work. Small workshops are therefore gradually being revived and offering further outlets for designers and craftsmen.

So-called 'artist-craftsmen' should not incidentally be confused with reproductive craftsmen. A 'reproductive' craftsman, in any field, is one who in general copies or reproduces, often with considerable skill, someone else's idea. An artist or designer-craftsman is not just the executant, but is also responsible for the original idea.

The crafts revival

The recent revival in crafts has, of course, taken many forms and is not only manifest in the growing range of outlets such as small galleries and craft shops attracting tourist and other buyers. The rural crafts have in many areas had much attention given to them and the urban, industrial crafts—such as silversmithing, clock making and book binding—are also, in some cases, beginning to return to our cities.

The traditional crafts are however by no means all associated with the country. Man has been living in towns for a long time and developed many hand and industrial crafts which need busy city life and workshop space.

Primarily however we have changed from a hand—craft based society, where we do not 'do and make' anymore, but where a designer plans and the machine makes. Working as a designer is therefore predominant in terms of job opportunities but craft and design, like art and design, go hand in hand both during the training of the designer and throughout his professional career.

It is interesting that groups of craftsmen are gradually moving back into towns and cities from where they had previously been banished as part of so-called 'urban development'. The revival of urban craft workshops provides further evidence that opportunities and outlets for designers continue to be found in both industrial production and craftwork. Both areas should not be polarised and seen as totally incompatible for both can play a part in providing work for artists and in producing designed artifacts for all manner of markets.

4   How do artists, designers and craftsmen work – what do they do?

Work in art and design depends largely on individual ability and personality and it therefore follows that every artist or designer tends to establish his or her own style and character of work. Some of the work that artists and designers undertake is within the organised framework of industry and may therefore follow an ordered pattern, while other work may be done with the artist working on his own, with the nature of the job varying with each commission.

Although we have seen that the work of artists, designers and craftsmen is in fact closely interwoven, it may help, in generalised terms, to briefly, and rather artificially, look separately at how they work.

Artists

Most painters and sculptors work on their own, either producing work which has been commissioned by a client, or developing their own ideas which they then hope to sell through art dealers or galleries.

The market for fine art work is particularly subject to changes in fashion and the economy generally. Today's society, as a whole, probably has less direct need for painters and sculptors than previous periods of history. We tend not to need so many painted portraits, statues and painted records of events than were required in an age before photography, film and television. However, the nature of commissions for fine artists has changed, as has fine art as an activity, and we now often find sculptors and painters commissioned to work in other media such as film and television, the theatre and new building projects. The flow of commissions for the fine artist, however varied, are however not likely to form a continuous source of income, unless the artist is particularly specialised in a narrow field (such as portraiture), or renowned and in demand.

Fine artists must therefore, like designers, be tenacious and willing to diversify and work in all manner of associated fields where their creative capacities are needed. All manner of

The artist, designer and craftsperson in society

industries need creative ideas and fine artists often work in association with the theatre, music, publishing and entertainment industries, to name just a few.

Rather than work totally in response to commissions, even if they are available, most fine artists are concerned with developing their own ideas and hopefully inventing or finding a market or outlet for them.

This clearly, while very worthwhile, is a precarious operation in terms of earning a living. Any outlet for such work is very much related to individual talent, fashion and luck, and most artists working in this way need to find some way of supplementing their income. Teaching, particularly part-time, has in the past offered many painters a basis from which they can find time to develop their ideas, but recent cuts in the education service have made this less easy.

Fine artists therefore, in simple terms, need patrons. The nature of patronage has clearly changed throughout history; at one time large wealthy families and royalty may have employed artists and at other times the prosperous merchant classes. Today all manner of people and organisations patronise or try and support fine artists in a variety of ways. The state, in employing artists as teachers, has helped many artists, in the past, survive and earn time to paint and develop their ideas. Local authorities in developing, for example, community art centres and using artists to paint murals and help in urban renewal, also contribute to employing artists. Large industries of all kinds are, in varying degrees, also often patrons of the arts. They may commission artists, or sponsor exhibitions, or offer scholarships or bursaries to help artists develop and survive. We now also have national organisations, like the Arts Council, supported by central government, set up to support the work of artists.

Whatever the nature of sponsorship and patronage the life of the fine artist remains a precarious affair which should not be contemplated unless you are very talented, committed and personally determined.

Designers

Design careers, and the work of the designer, cover a wide variety of specialisations and different jobs. There are so many types of products, for different purposes (ranging from printed fabrics to garden forks, and from saucepans to record covers and from jet engines or road signs to an entire hospital or a simple pair of scissors), that the designer's work always varies.

In what is generally known as industrial design, the designer is largely concerned with the *appearance* of the product and the way people use it. Alternatively, the engineering designer is mainly concerned with the *performance* of the product. Clearly the roles of performance and appearance overlap and this is one of the reasons why designers usually work, or consult with, groups of people concerned with different aspects of the product.

The industrial or product designer is however, in broad terms, largely concerned with the visual appearance of objects (often dictated by mechanical function) and is therefore trained in an art college. The engineering designer, concerned with the mechanical operation and performance, has a different training. In both cases however the designer will need a knowledge of materials and manufacturing methods and to bear in mind such important factors as cost, safety, maintenance and users' requirements.

Designers mostly work in one or two ways. They are either employed on the staff of industrial or commercial companies and public corporations, or they may operate on their own or in small groups as freelance consultants.

'Staff' designers, or those employed full-time by a company, work in a design office, usually alongside other designers concerned with designing the products of the particular firm, while freelance designers or consultants take work from a range of companies in whatever field they may be working.

Designers therefore either work from their own homes or offices, or go to work in a design office for a particular company. A great majority of designed products are produced by freelance or consultant designers, but young designers, in the early stages of their careers, tend more to work in design offices before branching out into private practice. It does however depend on the type of industry. Some industries, by the nature of their product, need many staff designers while other industries find it more economic, or appropriate, to go outside their company and employ designers on a freelance basis.

The design process normally begins with the designer discussing what is required with the client or his representative. If the designer is a freelance consultant, he will do this direct with the client, whereas if he is a staff designer his discussions will be with someone in the firm.

What is wanted may be an entirely new product, or possibly, more commonly, a small but important modification to an existing product. The designer then starts 'putting down' his ideas, usually sketching his design proposals or making models or experiments to check whether his idea works.

When the sketch, model, or first prototype has been tested and agreed the designer then works with others such as design assistants, technicians, craftworkers or model makers, on the final production prototype and drawings which form the instructions to those who will produce and manufacture the product.

This brief and generalised description of the designers work shows that other specialists work alongside a designer, particularly specialist craftsmen, technical assistants and model makers. These allied technician careers have their own vocational training, either at an art or technical college.

It is also possibly worth pointing out at this stage that a great deal of design work is concerned with modifications to existing products rather than totally new products. Clearly design work varies from industry to industry but 'tooling up' for a completely new product is expensive and once a product is produced it has to have a long life to justify the outlay. Entirely new products are therefore more rare than modifications but it does depend on the nature of the product. For instance, some industries, such as, printing and advertising, are concerned with ephemeral products —that is products which do not have a long life; we throw away our bus tickets, football programmes and magazines and constantly need new ones. Similarly the life of an advertisement or package may by very short. Fashion trends and economics obviously play a part in this, but it is important, when considering the designers' work, to remember that the products of some industries have short lives, and designers are more frequently needed to redesign new images or products, while other industries call less frequently on the work of the designer as their products, for many reasons, have a much longer life span.

In taking a general look at the work of the designer it is important to stress at this stage that all design work and training is open equally to both men and women. Some trades and industries have traditions which seem to suggest that one profession is more of a male or female province, such as fashion for girls and industrial design for boys. But any such stereotype attitudes should be rigorously resisted. Training opportunities are certainly equal.

If we remember that everything around us that is man-made has been designed by someone, then we can begin to realise that the work of the designer encompasses many activities. The jobs closest to art and design training include, for example, the work of the graphic designer, textiles and fashion designer and three-dimensional or industrial product designer—all are concerned primarily with the way things look and work—that is the shape, feel, form, colour and size of all the products we use. But shape and appearance cannot be separated from function and there are many elements of the designer's work outside visual style and appearance.

The artist, designer and craftsperson in society

Parallel to the work of the industrial or visual designer is the work of the engineering designer. This book is concerned primarily with work in art and design, but it is necessary to realise the enormous breadth and complexity of design activity including the role of the engineering designer.

Engineering design, for example, covers the production of trains, nuclear reactors, computers, telecommunication systems, and all manner of vehicles and machines, together with mechanical and power tools; to say nothing of mechanical components such as gears, engines, screws, nuts and bolts. Engineering design includes the two specialist fields of mechanical engineering design and electronic engineering design, and many other specialist areas ranging from production engineering design to civil, marine and aeronautical engineering design.

It is clear from such a list that some products are designed more by engineers and others by industrial or product designers. Design responsibilities frequently overlap and different kinds of designers often work together to ensure that appearance, technical performance and mechanical operation are all equally considered.

Experts from the different disciplines, particularly industrial and engineering design, will therefore be involved and work together on the design. Each specialist has his own area of responsibility, using his particular skills and training, and concentrating on a different aspect of the whole product.

This consultative process, with different specialists working together as a group, in a sense typifies design activity. Unlike the disciplines of fine art and craft, design in essence is a group activity depending, to a large degree, on designers consulting with other specialists, considering ideas from other people, and seeing their work as part of the total production process. By contrast the fine artist and craftsman tend to work more in isolation with the complete process of production undertaken by them.

Craftsmen

Alongside the artist and designer is the craftsman. The craftsman, and woman, combine in their work many of the characteristics of both the artist and designer. As has already been shown we need to use the phrase 'artist-craftsman' or 'designer-crafsman' to distinguish between the creative craftsman, who designs and makes, and the purely 'reproductive craftsman' who executes or copies someone else's design, or plan.

Craft work is a more personal business than that of design, with the craftsman usually working alone, or in a small workshop or studio, in a traditional activity such as ceramics, jewellery,

The artist, designer and craftsperson in society

woodwork or weaving. Many production processes and industries have both a craft and an industrial tradition. For example, ceramics was initially a hand craft which has become industrialised but still supports a hand craft industry. Alternatively, some new materials, such as plastics, have no craft tradition and new industries, like electronics, similarly have no industrial craft background. So craftsmen work mainly in traditional processes and materials and unlike the designer, who is concerned with multiple production, the craftworker makes single individual pieces.

Craftwork is produced outside any mass industrial production system and without the support of advertising and a market structure with national outlets. Unlike industrial products, craftwork is sold in limited numbers from the premises of the craftsman, or direct to retailers, if they have not been commissioned privately. Working totally as a craftsman can bring with it some of the difficulties, in terms of commissions and patronage, that the fine artist experiences.

Craftsmen usually have to deal with all aspects of the production process from the original idea, or discussion with the client, through all the 'rough work' stages of working out and testing the idea through to the completed product. The product then has to be marketed, 'advertised', transported and sold by the craftsman. In fact he probably also has to keep his own accounts; all this is rather removed from the work of the staff designer in industry who operates as part of the production team with specialists responsible for every stage.

The late Sir Gordon Russell (the first Director of the Design Council) in his book *The Story of Furniture* gives a splendid example of all the jobs a craftsman might have to do.

'Bill Battersby (chairmaker) used to go to a near-by coppice where he knew good straight ash-poles were growing. He selected a number, marked them with white paint, and bought them standing from the farmer who owned the coppice. To-day he would have been called (Timber Merchant). Then with his son he cut them down (Timber Feller), and carted them to his workshop (Haulier). Arrived there, he split some up with wedges and sawed others in a saw-pit (Sawyer). He then stacked some to season (Labourer), and others he turned while green (Turner) to designs which he had evolved by trial and error over a long period (Industrial Designer). He then assembled the parts (Chairmaker), and rushed the seats (Upholsterer). Finally, he stained and polished them (Polisher). He then loaded them onto a cart (Packer), and took them to the nearest market town (Carter). Arrived there, he set up, a stall in the market-place (Advertiser), and set them out (Shop-keeper). He sold them (Salesman) and received the money (Cashier). He then went to the Red Lion for a well earned pot of beer.

The artist, designer and craftsperson in society

In the bar he met his customers in a friendly way and listened to their approval or complaints (Public Relations Officer and Marketing Research Group). Finally, he went home with various orders in his head or on odd slips of paper (traveller). These he put in a teapot on the mantel-shelf, to be taken out as required (Book-keeper).'

Of course this referred to a pre-industrial society but it illustrated how a craftsman, working on his own, might have to undertake all manner of things. Designers of course also often work on their own and sometimes see more of the whole production process than some staff designers working full-time in a company's design office. What is important to stress is the wide range of roles and activities and how they overlap. We have already seen how a designer can also work as a craftsman and throughout his career these roles can fluctuate in emphasis, depending on the type of work a craftsman-designer undertakes.

The craftsman is in one sense halfway between the fine artist and the designer. The craftsman's work, like the painter, starts with his own idea, and it is this idea that he develops and expresses, whereas the designer responds to someone else's needs or a client's commission. Craftsmen can also of course, from time to time, work to a design commission and on such occasions operate in much the same way as an industrial or product designer.

There is clearly still a very important role for craftwork and many of the products we use, from knitwear and ceramics to jewellery and beautiful glassware are the products of hand craftsmen. Their work clearly enriches and extends the range of goods available, giving consumers an alternative choice to the mass products of industry.

5 The growth of the design profession – professional bodies and the art schools

Design as a profession, and in fact as a word in general usage, is very much a product of the twentieth century. In a pre-industrial society the work of designing and making were not separated. There was no such thing as an industrial designer; there were craftsmen and workmen who made things and they also happened to decide what these things looked like. They either followed patterns and traditions passed down from generation to generation or worked out the shape of things themselves through long experience, trial and error, and finding out what shapes were most effective; which were cheapest, strongest, and most pleasing.

With mass production and the growth of technology, specialist activities developed and the role of the craftsman became separated from the designer. As the demand for more things and

The artist, designer and craftsperson in society

bigger things grew no one person could do all the jobs. No one, for instance, could design and make a steamship, or large machine or railway engine, and as industrialisation developed design gradually became a separate drawing office activity and making and designing were largely divided. The industrial designer is therefore very much a product of this century—it is one of the new, and exciting professions, of twentieth century technology. In fact we could rightly say that industrial design is the art of the twentieth century and the most significant activity and profession to have grown out of our age. It is in part the process of giving consumer goods, from cars to fountain pens, and all man-made things, an industrial identity or 'look'. This is not to say that the look of things is the most important part of a designed object, but it is that part which we see, and which influences so dramatically the world around us.

It is therefore very significant that art schools, or faculties of art and design are responsible for the training of most industrial designers. It is the professional training in visual form that underpins the ultimate shape and form of things. The education of the visual sense for the designer clearly does not reside exclusively in art training and many famous engineers and architects did not necessarily go to art school, though they certainly had strong visual sense and skills. However, the tradition of art school work and training has no doubt contributed massively to the growth of industrial design as a profession. Without doubt drawing as an activity is fundamental to the work of designers—it is the method by which we give form and shape to our ideas and art schools are certainly the major institutions providing the training in this and many other skills that the designer needs.

When Henry Cole sert up the first Government Schools of Drawing, after the 1851 Great Exhibition in which he played such an important part, the stated aim was 'to encourage and give those skills to develop the manufacturing arts'. Art schools sprang up all over the country in the last half of the nineteenth centry all concerned with developing skills in art which would support the emerging new manufacturing industries. This however was applying fine art to manufactured goods not training the artist in the disciplines and skills of design.

The evolution of art schools during the present century has reflected the changing function of artists in society with a very considerable extension of the range of activities taught. At one time (in fact probably up to the 1930s) drawing and sculpture, related to a fine art tradition, were the main, and only, activities of art schools, with occasional additions of certain studio crafts such as pottery and weaving.

The artist, designer and craftsperson in society

The largest single factor of change in the last forty years or so has been the recognition of 'design' as a necessary area of study in its own right and no longer an occasional by-product of fine art training. Design training is therefore now a major element of art school work and deceptively simple words like 'art' and 'design' now cover a vast range of activities and skills relating to the design profession. While art schools have therefore grown and extended their work to cover the training of industrial designers in almost all fields, so the designer's work itself has broadened and become more specialised.

Designers have therefore organised their work and developed professional organisations to support them and encourage and oversee the training for the profession. The growth of 'professionalism' is very much part of the twentieth century and all the new professions have established their professional institutions, for example, the Institute of Civil Engineers and the Institute of Mechanical Engineers.

The Society of Industrial Artists and Designers has its origins a little later but is now a professional body to which most designers belong, and which supports designers and establishes professional codes of practice and involves itself with the training and education of designers. Artists and designers, like other professionals, need the support of professional bodies and institutions. But designers, craftsmen and artists need probably more support as the job structure for craftsmen and designers is not so easily safeguarded and indentified.

The work of artists, designers and craftsmen is, as we've seen, subject to fashion and patronage and the fluctuations of national wealth. Too often art and design is seen incorrectly as a luxury and frequently designers have to stress the importance of design and fight for recognition. As a society we do not always realise how vitally important design is, not only to our well being and surroundings, but to our success as an industrial nation.

The artist, craftsman and designer, as a relative newcomer to the industrial stage, therefore need support and encouragement. Professional bodies have therefore grown up to assist designers and a whole range of national organisations have developed during this century to promote the vital work of the designer. All these are listed on page 142 but of particular importance are the Design Council developing from the Design and Industries Association, the Crafts Council growing from the Crafts Advisory Council and of course the Arts Council itself. These bodies along with the Society of Industrial Artists and Designers, and Rural Industries Board, have developed during the century to sponsor the arts and crafts and help give support to artists and designers and, most important of all bring the work of the designer, artist-craftsman to the attention of the public.

2 Before you go to art school

1 Can anyone be an artist?

The professions of Art and Design can be described as a 'talent' and 'fashion' industry. By that we mean you need a real and genuine talent for visual and practical work and for the expression of ideas in visual form; and that much of the industry or profession is subject to the world of changing fashion trends.

Talent or ability can of course be developed, in fact many professionals are suspicious of the idea of any in-born talent or any sense of 'creative gift'. This may or not be so, but what is clear is that you will need to have real ability in art and then have to develop that ability into an exceptional talent by hard work. Many people who have shown some aptitude for art at school think vaguely about 'taking up art'. The commitment and talent required to succeed in art and design is such that you should dismiss it from your mind if it is something vague and only a casual interest, or something you are 'quite good at'.

To be successful, and establish yourself in a competitive field, it is necessary to have above average ability and more important an almost passionate commitment to drawing, painting and making things; and to all things related to the world of art and design. Without this commitment and enthusiasm, at the expense of other interests, you should possibly not even contemplate a career in art and design, particularly in any area associated with fine arts. Not only is the profession competitive and dependent on high levels of personal creative ability, it is also, as already suggested, influenced by changing fashions, trends and tastes. Not all aspects of the work of the craftsman, artist and designer are affected by fashion changes but it should be recognised that the fluctuations in demand, and changes in public taste, make very real demands on a professional during his or her career. While it can be a wonderfully rewarding way of life, disappointments should be expected which can only be tolerated if the artist has a real sense of commitment and could not possibly do anything else. You should not need to be told whether to study art but know in yourself that no other career is possible for you.

Before you go to art school

It is therefore evident that not anyone can be an artist or designer. A passing interest in the subject is not sufficient, you have to be able to practise and perform your skills, so talent and ability are essential if you are hoping to train as a practising professional. The fact that artists and designers actually make things and draw and put their ideas into practise is important. As a practising artist or designer you need the skills to perform professionally; a passive interest in art is insufficient. If you have a strong interest in art but no practical ability then there are relevant jobs for you in associated fields, but not as a practitioner. Of course a talent in art is valuable in itself and can be developed for personal pleasure and satisfaction. Such a talent can enrich our lives and can contribute to many careers which appear to have no connection with art.

How you know whether you have the necessary abilities and what particular qualities are required for specific disciplines is explored later in this chapter but the simple answer is to seek professional advice to the extent of your talent either from your art teacher or local art school.

2 Is training necessary?

In general there are no opportunities in art and design for school leavers without professional training. Entry to the profession is through specialist training at a school or college of art or a faculty of art and design in a polytechnic or college of higher education. There are, as always, the exceptions. No doubt a few very talented and exceptional people have somehow developed a unique natural talent and become artists without formal training but these must be extremely rare. There are also some limited training opportunities in industry for young people direct from school, but these are strictly speaking not in the area of creative design but usually in the ancillary supporting technical occupations. For example, there are limited opportunities for training as a technical draughtsman but such work is not as a designer but rather supporting the designer in the translation of his ideas into production. In other words, to be a creative designer and actually determine what products should look like, is a professional occupation needing professional training. Most supporting occupations, such as design technician and model maker or pattern cutter also need specialist training; so it is accurate to assume that there is, broadly speaking, no entry into art and design occupations without proper further training. Though as in all professions a few people manage, by exceptional ability and determination, to succeed without having been through a formal training, or by learning their trade completely on the workshop floor.

Before you go to art school

Primarily, training is concerned with developing skills and ability through practical experience. Subsequent work and employment is obtained on the evidence of the standard of work produced, not so much on the level of award in a degree or diploma. However, particularly in specialised fields of design, professional qualifications are becoming more important, and specialist knowledge and new technologies have to be learned alongside the development of practical skills. Designers of course get jobs or commissions, in a competitive world, on the basis of being able to show clients how good their actual work is. But qualifications within the profession are being taken more seriously and a combination of a good degree or diploma, together with evidence of practical skills and creative ability, is the objective of good design training.

3 What reasons may you have for choosing art?

The real and probably only sensible reason for choosing art and design is that you want to do it more than anything else. Anything less than that sense of commitment could prove disastrous in what is a highly competitive profession where the vagaries of personal choice, talent and fashion can make life very hard for all but the most devoted and tenacious person.

However, it may help to look at some other reasons for considering a career in art and design. One reason (if it could be called that), which should be dismissed immediately, is the misguided idea that art and design is an 'easy option', avoiding hard work and academic rigour. This misunderstanding sometimes comes from schools where art is sadly only treated as a soft option and is seen as an unimportant subject. Art in schools all too often unfortunately has this 'luxury' image. Nothing could of course be further from the truth. Training in art and design is long and rigorous and entry both to colleges and any subsequent employment is competitive. The demands made at all levels are considerable in terms of intellectual, technical and creative abilities and any negative reason for choosing art and design as an easy option would be extremely foolish, though such a lack of commitment would no doubt be revealed at the first interview for a college place.

The most common reason for considering a career in art and design is obviously because you are good at it and it is one of your better subjects in school. This is a sound reason and coincides with the need for a high level of individual talent. However, you may have considerable natural ability but not find much success in the subject at school. This may be because you have been forced to

Before you go to art school

drop the subject due to the examination arrangements at your school or that the provision for art in your school does not help your particular talents. This is where real commitment and personal initiative are necessary (the very qualities needed in a creative, imaginative designer), for you then have to get advice and work on your own, using your free time to continue developing your interest in art. There is a difference between the art taught in secondary schools and the level and objectives of professional training, and being forced to drop art in school should not necessarily deter the determined and potentially gifted from working his or her way through.

A further reason, possibly worth considering, though only as a supporting and confirming factor (in addition to the logical sense of just wanting to do nothing else), is the potential, personal satisfaction associated with any creative work. In an industrial society much work is becoming de-personalised, repetitive, and anonymous, and the opportunity to express oneself, create something new, and actually determine the shape and form of things, is clearly very attractive. More and more people are looking for meaningful work through which expression can be given to individual ideas and concepts and this is no doubt one reason why courses in art and design are normally heavily oversubscribed and very popular.

Art and design certainly offers opportunities for personal expression and individuality and provides us with the chance to see if 'our ideas work'. In this sense art school training is of considerable educational value in its own right irrespective of any vocational outlets on the completion of training. However, although this sense of obvious creative job satisfaction is attractive it is not a feasible reason in itself without the personal ability and skills to actually be able to reach the necessary high professional standards required for employment.

The quality of education, personal development and creative experience gained through an art education is of immense value to individuals, and many might argue that it is one of the most positive forms of liberalising education available in its own right. This in fact is probably so but the prime objective of higher education in art and design is vocational—meaning that it is directed to a specific vocation or job. The fact that it also incorporates processes of self discovery and creative development is in a sense an inherent bonus.

This therefore brings us to a final further reason for considering a career in art, namely employment in a specific occupation and so-called job security. It is important to remember that when choosing any course in art and design, or any other subject that

Before you go to art school

there is no *guarantee* of a job at the end of it. The job market is always unpredictable and in art and design it varies from subject to subject, and is influenced not only by economic fluctuation but changes in fashion and public taste. Surprisingly the record for employing graduates in art and design in jobs appropriate to their training, is higher than many people imagine and certainly at present not markedly worse than the majority of other vocational subjects. The important point to remember is that basically a craftsman-artist or designer has to find a market for his ideas and the hard reality is that in a sense you have to *invent your own existence*. Certain types of jobs are advertised, particularly design office jobs in areas of industrial design, graphics, advertising and other fields of design closely associated with industry. But outside these design areas the world of a freelance designer and artist-craftsman is one in which your ability and ideas have to be attractive and you have to go out and sell your ideas, establish an interest in your ability, and create or find your own market. Although for many it is a rewarding and well paid career, it does mean you have to sell your ability and go and find the work, it's not out there waiting for you. This may of course put many people off and is a further reason for stressing the need for initially possessing sufficient genuine ability and having a capacity for real hard work. The job market for those with real talent and original ideas is, however, good, but job security is another thing. Again the situation varies according to each specialist area. Designers employed full-time by companies can usually enjoy the normal expectations of regular employment, while freelance designers and craftsmen are more subject to changes in public demand and fashion. A student, for example, may obtain an interesting commission on leaving college and appear, as it were, to be 'set up' (this often happens as a young student may offer something new to the market—and that is what employers and the public want) but as fashions change their ideas may not be so acceptable in a few years' time and different ideas may then be needed.

The working life of an artist-designer does not always follow a continuous progression but is influenced by the 'ups and downs' in the market and the changing demand for what he or she can produce. Artists and designers must therefore be constantly aware of changing trends and be able always to develop new ideas.

Much of what has been said about so-called job prospects could of course be said about any subject and it may be worth returning to the point that art and design education offers a most worthwhile personal form of education with, in many cases, an honours degree at the end, which in itself is intrinsically valuable.

Having pointed out some of the very real difficulties it should

Before you go to art school

however be stressed that art and design, both as a form of education and as a creative way of life, offers the opportunity for much personal happiness and creative expression. Artists and designers are not only privileged in being able to do what they want to do, and enjoy the rich personal benefits associated with creating and making things, but they also have the benefit of being involved in self-discovery and expression. Artists and designers are trained to look at the world with imagination and critical perception and it is in this, together with being able actually to have a say in how things look, and in making new things, that makes it such an attractive way of life.

4 What abilities and skills are needed?

We have already stressed the need for above average ability in art and a real sense of personal commitment, combined with talent and a capacity for hard work. But what actual abilities are needed by an artist and designer and how important is the role of drawing? Talents may take many forms; the ability to draw, sensitivity to colour, shape and form, skill in handling materials and making things and the ability to learn new techniques and see the potential of new technologies. In addition designers need an enquiring and analytical mind, the ability to get on with people, and possibly some mathematical, scientific and even linguistic knowledge. Above all you need a sense of real curiosity, and creative imagination combined with an interest in people and the world in which we live. You also need a lot of resilience, perseverence and, along with hard work, the capacity to believe in yourself and your ideas.

This section sets out to explore these points and look particularly at the different skills needed by the artist and the designer.

It has already been established that, though they overlap, the separate activities of art and design differ. A major difference is in motivation and methods of working. The fine artist and craftsman often work alone developing their own ideas while the designer has to deal with external problems and work with other people. Fine artists have to find and develop a way of working which is appropriate to the development of their own ideas, while the designer has to find ways of working which meet the demands made on him by the problem he is solving and the brief he has been given by the client.

One common activity for both the artist and the designer is however the ability to draw, but there are many kinds of drawing. We sometimes think that drawing is only concerned with picture making, depicting scenes and obtaining a 'likeness'. This is a very

Before you go to art school

narrow view of drawing. More fundamentally drawing is concerned with communicating ideas and information visually. This can take many different forms. All artists, designers and craftsmen need to convey information visually and put their ideas on paper in different ways, and drawing is certainly the underlying basic activity for much design work. We use drawing to show other people, including the client, what our ideas may look like, we also use drawing to inform the manufacturer or technical craftsman how to make up something we have designed and we use drawing to help us observe, analyse and understand the world around us. Fine artists may use drawing to express ideas and we all may in fact use it in different ways.

Drawing is therefore part of all work in art and design, but ideas can be communicated and information collected in other ways and the real skill is that which allows us to communicate our ideas visually to other people. The most common way of doing this happens to be drawing on paper, but this can mean anything from a detailed sketch to a chart or diagram.

Photography and other forms of collecting and conveying visual material are useful, but however varied our approach, some form of drawing or visual communication skill is important.

It may help to dwell on the broader idea of 'visual skill', for drawing may suggest too narrow an activity when what is required is an ability to convey information visually in whatever way is appropriate.

Some form of visual skill is therefore essential to the artist and designer, but we equally need to be practical and good at 'making'—this could be described as 'practical skills'.

Artists not only give form to their ideas in two-dimensions but also work in three-dimensions and a wide range of materials. Design is, in part, about giving form and shape to our ideas, and practical skills in manipulating a wide range of materials are essential. Some ideas are best communicated in solid form and much of the designed world, from fashion through to furniture design, is three-dimensional. Our ability to manipulate and work practically with materials is essential and we need to have an aptitude for forming and shaping and for modelling our ideas. Ideas can be expressed in all manner of ways, in fact there are as many ways as there are people and materials, but two-dimensional and three-dimensional forms are the most usual ways of putting our ideas into action.

In summary, therefore, artists and designers need skills in communicating ideas in both two- and three-dimensions, in drawing and making, in other words the visual and practical skills. So fundamentally you will need to be good with your hands and have an acute visual sense.

Rather than think of these skills as exceptional gifts or talents, it may help to consider the idea of having the ability to understand the language of form and the language of vision. They are in fact languages in that designers and artists convey ideas and information through vision and form and therefore need to be articulate in terms of design and visual literacy.

In addition to visual and practical skills artists and designers need to possess a strong sense of curiosity and invention. All creative work is basically about problem solving, and to solve problems you need skills of analysis, curiosity and invention. Problem solving is a very fundamental activity concerned with identifying a problem, proposing a solution and then testing the solution to see if it works. To be successful at this you need to combine analytical skills with the ability of imaginative curiosity—you have to say 'this is my idea—let's see if it works'.

A great deal of work connected with art and design and problem solving, requires that difficult to define commodity, 'originality'. It can be identified or described in problem solving as the 'hitherto unseen solution to a problem' but more often it is that quality of personality which makes each of us different from other people. The development of personal curiosity and a lively original response to problems is therefore a further requirement when looking for potential artists and designers.

Much of what has so far been explored relates to both the fine artist and designer. If your aptitude lies in the field of fine art you will certainly need the personal skills of self expression and a high level of ability in personal problem solving. You will also need exceptional talent in drawing, painting and possibly modelling, but such creative talents will be personal to you, whereas the designer has to work in a much broader context.

Design combines so-called artistic sensitivity with a need to solve technical problems and an essential capacity to discuss both problems and solutions with other people.

Designers work in a team, as part of a production process, and have therefore to understand other people's points of view and their specialist disciplines—this calls for an ability to work with other people and to see problems from their point of view. The designer must also be methodical in his approach—time and money are important aspects of design production, and designers cannot leave work until they feel in the right 'creative mood'. Design, being concerned with production, means that the process must fit in with schedules and the designer needs the ability to combine so-called creative flair with business sense and orderliness. The designer not only has to design what his or her

Before you go to art school

employer requires, meeting deadlines and budgets, he has also to be responsible for taking into account the needs of the people who will use his product.

Considering 'product use' is a very convenient way of highlighting some of the different qualities needed as an artist and a designer. Paintings and pieces of sculpture are not 'used' in the same way as the objects produced by the designer and it is the ability of the designer to make sure that his product works which calls for an analytical attitude and sense of caring detail.

Not much has so far been said about the specific abilities needed by craftsmen as, in a sense, craft combines the attributes required in both the designer and fine artist. However, one further requirement is the ability to make things well—this is one of the practical skills which all artists and designers need. Craftsmen, who are responsible for the total production process, particularly need the skill and patience to see a job through to the highest standard of finish. This element of caring professionalism or of 'doing a job well' is also a fundamental requirement for the aspiring artist or designer. The ultimate objective for all craftsmen, artists or designers is ideally to do a job well, whether it is made by hand or machine. Towards this end we may use 'rough work' in the sense of a sketch or working model, to develop our idea and see if it works. But whatever we produce has to have a quality of professional finish or of performing its function properly—that is what practical skills, in one sense, are about.

For all branches of art and design you will need personal conviction, tenacity to see the job through, and the ability to get on well with people, for so much design work involves teamwork and co-operation.

Finally, if one can imagine art and design as a broad spectrum running from fine art and painting at one end to heavy technical industrial design at the other end then we can begin to realise the range of different skills needed. The 'fine art' end of our spectrum obviously calls for more personal creativity and individual expressive talent, particularly in drawing and painting, while the other extreme of industrial design calls for more analytical and technical skills (including even mathematics and physics) with a varying combination of these abilities in the middle.

5 From secondary school to art school

(i) Why a foundation course?
In terms of studying art and design there is a large gap between work at secondary school level and higher and further education. The difference between the two levels of work needs some

Before you go to art school

exploration as it clearly affects pupils moving on to professional training.

Art and design as a profession covers a very wide range of specialisations. Simple words like 'art' and 'design' now represent a vast range of activities and skills. Working in art and design, and study for the profession, includes subjects, for example, as diverse as fine art, design management, carpet design, industrial design, film making, textile technology and work with all manner of materials.

The expansion of the concept and practise of art and design has obviously not been matched in schools, many of which are unable to extend their art and design coverage beyond general drawing, painting and simple craft activities. Young pupils therefore find it difficult to judge or assess their aptitude for the complex world of art and design as they are unlikely to have had any experience of many of the specialist disciplines associated with the field. How, for example, does the average fifth or sixth former know if he has any real aptitude for working in plastics or as a graphic designer or in jewellery, shoe design, film making or the complex world of product design?

There is therefore a big difference between the breadth of art and design as a professional subject and the narrow coverage available in schools. Such a gap would not offer too many problems if specialisation in training was not necessary. The simple truth however is that if the young designer is to be employable at the end of his training he must specialise. Art and design is a competitive profession in which talent and technical skills must be developed to a high level if they are to be any use in the employment market—subject specialisation is therefore essential. Or, to put it another way, if your ideas and standard of work are going to be worth buying at the end of your training then you need to concentrate on one subject, or a narrow range, throughout your training. This leap from a few basic crafts, and some drawing and painting in schools, to the problem of selecting an area for career specialisation is a problem specific to art and design. You are unlikely to know, without experience, where your specific aptitudes lie and yet you cannot afford to spend too much precious study time moving from one specialisation to another. Art and design education overcomes this problem by what is known as a *Foundation* course (or what used to be called a pre-diploma or introductory course). This course is usually of one year's duration and sets out primarily to be diagnostic. By this is meant that the student is, as it were, exposed throughout the year to the widest possible range of materials and processes to find out or 'diagnose' where his or her real aptitude lies.

Before you go to art school

From a foundation course a student then moves on to specialist degree or diploma course study. A student at secondary school cannot, from experience, know whether he has the necessary interest or skills to develop as a specialist designer in a specific field, so it is absolutely crucial that foundation courses play this important role in helping the student to find out.

In a sense the foundation course is like a year long interview at which the student finds out about himself. Tutors can observe and guide in appropriate directions, and contact can be made with all manner of potential specialist areas so that informed application, based on real experience, may be made to subsequent specialist training. The foundation course therefore provides a bridge between school and high level professional training and is where decisions should be made about future specialisation and finding out where your talents lie. School experience, however good, cannot normally provide sufficient breadth to give a basis for making such judgements. Professional training is expensive both in terms of time (at least three to four years) and resources and students cannot enter a specialist field just thinking or hoping it's the right one for them. It sometimes takes a long time to find out where your real talent lies. Not only do real abilities in art take some time to develop, but also you may be compensating for having done very little art and design at school—as it is not often a priority subject for the academically able—as our education tends to give more prominence to words and theory than doing and making. Using the foundation course as a vehicle for 'finding out' is also sensible in economic terms. Students in art and design (and other subjects) are awarded up to three years of mandatory grants for study on degrees and diplomas. It is important not to waste one of these years by being on a course in the wrong specialism. A foundation course does not however merit a mandatory award, you only get a 'discretionary' grant for such pre-degree courses. This means you usually live at home and have some discretionary financial help from your local education authority, with your mandatory three-year grant untouched. Therefore, to put it another way, should you decide after a foundation course that you are not suited for further specialist training then you could go on to alternative subject study in higher education not having used up any of your mandatory three-years grant allocation.

(ii) When do I decide?
More will be said about foundation courses in the next chapter but the critical point to remember, at this stage, is that decisions about specific career specialisations should be left until you are actually on a foundation course.

Before you go to art school

Many young students have an idea of what they may want to do when they are still at school. It is however almost impossible to make an informed decision without knowledge and experience of the specialism. Foundation courses will not usually be expecting specialist career decisions to have been made at the time of your interview. What will be looked for is a general ability and potential in art and design with the decision on specialist future training delayed until you are on the foundation course.

Decisions about specialisation may therefore be left until you are actually on a pre-degree or pre-diploma course, but deciding when to leave school, and deciding generally on a career in art and design, is another problem.

As we will see in the next chapter there are a wide range of courses which can be started at different ages. There are Certificate courses that 16 year olds can join and Diplomas which you can enter at 17 or 18 and degree courses which you can only commence from the age of 18 onwards.

Individual cases for leaving school vary and it is impossible to generalise. You can only decide by discussing it fully with teachers, parents and friends. 'O' and 'A' level passes are necessary for entry to most courses and although emphasis is put on the standard of your practical work and creative ability, your academic school qualifications are also important. In a competitive profession, including often severe competition for degree and diploma course places, it obviously can help having good 'O' and 'A' level passes.

Entry to courses is based on personal work shown in a folder and academic qualifications—it is, in a sense, therefore a balance between the two factors and while an excellent folder may compensate for low academic qualifications similarly good GCE passes can compensate for shortcomings in your folder.

So if you are happy at school then there are advantages to staying on to obtain the best possible qualifications. Not only is selection competitive but increasingly elements of training and work in the profession make intellectual demands on young artists and designers requiring a very good sound general education. The earliest age at which a pre-degree one-year foundation course can be entered is 17 and the majority of students are usually 18, so there is no mad rush to leave school.

Putting aside the consideration of GCE qualifications there is a further reason for not being too impatient to leave school and start training. Professional training is demanding and maturity of attitude and a certain self-discipline is necessary. The nature of art and design training makes particular demands on young students. Students are for example expected to work on their own, solve

Before you go to art school

their own problems, determine in part their own work projects and develop their own ideas. Work is no longer divided into small, easily digestible teaching periods, as at school. The pattern of creative development is therefore fairly rigorous, requiring personal qualities of organisation and imagination which frequently take some time to develop.

Genuine creative talent in art may also not develop or mature until the later stages at school. We all develop our abilities at varying rates and, while all very young children draw naturally and with spontaneity, this ability does not necessarily continue, and the more permanent creative talent, suited to professional training, may not emerge until much later. There is a real difference between the delightful natural creativity of young children and the critical analytical attitudes to materials and visual problems required for professional training. We must be sure that we are choosing the right career and the simple message is not to rush, but to take your time, and wait until your abilities and interests are so strong that you have an almost obsessive concern with all things related to design and the visual arts.

(iii) The folder of work
Entry to courses in terms of academic qualifications will be discussed in the next chapter. But whatever course you may apply for you will need to show examples of your work in a folder or portfolio and this will have to be prepared while you are still at school. Artists and designers need a folder, or portfolio of work, throughout their working lives. Art and design is about practical work and you have to show people 'what you can do' whether it is applying for a job, a college place, or meeting a prospective client.

As a school leaver it is clearly not sufficient to just say 'I want to do art'—you have to demonstrate that you have the necessary potential abilities and a folder of work has therefore to be taken with you to your interview—all applicants are interviewed, with their work, when applying for a college place.

Talents, abilities and interests vary according to each individual and different courses may require different specialist evidence, so it is not possible to set down a simple list of what is needed in all folders of work. It would be very easy to say, for example that every folder must contain so many still life drawings or paintings and a certain number of photographs or examples of craft work. Ability in art cannot be assessed in such a fixed way, it's not as easy as that. Art is about your individual abilities and talents and everyone is different so no narrow guidelines can be set out.

However some things are important. The folder must demonstrate the breadth of your interest and your basic drawing

Before you go to art school

ability. We have seen how drawing and visual communication are fundamental to work in art and design so it is clear that evidence of your ability to observe and analyse what you see is important. Equally, you need to provide evidence of your ability to put your ideas down clearly in whatever material or form is appropriate. Artists, as we know, usually communicate ideas through drawings, but they also use all manner of other materials—so the evidence of your visual skills may take many forms.

Similarly, you may need to show something of your practical skills—this may be in the form of models, constructions or craft work. This obviously can be photographed so you don't necessarily have to carry bulky objects around. Evidence of your practical and visual skills should therefore form the basis of your folder with the emphasis on your particular abilities, so it varies with each person.

In addition, it may help to distinguish between work done at school under supervision, or at least when the idea has been set as a project, and work undertaken on your own initiative. College interviewing staff will be looking for evidence of your own personal ideas, not those necessarily of your teacher, so while school work will no doubt form the bulk of your submission it helps to demonstrate that you are sufficiently committed to actually also work on your own; because it's that type of involvement that designers need.

The amount of work you put in your folder is another problem. Too much may not only be impossible to carry but may also not be sufficiently selective; while too little may not provide sufficient evidence of your potential. Art and design is about choosing and selecting—so how you select and arrange your folder is part of the process of demonstrating your ability. You need to select your work carefully to communicate clearly the range of your work, presenting it with a sense of order and efficiency. It is not just a process of throwing a few drawings into a folder but giving some thought to how best you can show the work you have done; in what sequence it may appear and how the work should be mounted or shown.

Some folders may even include examples of written work related to your studies in art and design, either explaining or supporting the evidence submitted. Notebooks, sketchbooks, visual diaries and scrapbooks should certainly be included as these all help to show how your ideas are developed. Working sketchbooks which show the development of an idea from original observation and rough sketches, to the final realisation, should form a critical part of your work and would naturally appear in your folder—just as they are used, without being artificially 'tidied up'. Your art teacher will no doubt advise you and help you begin to develop the important skill, that we all need, of putting a folder of work together.

(iv) What other preparations can I make before going to college?
Preparing for a college interview, or for entry into college, is not just a case of getting a folder of work together and obtaining a number of GCE passes. There are many helpful things you can do, including for example discovering as much about your local college, and work in art schools, as possible.

In addition to formal interviews most colleges offer advisory interviews where prospective students can visit the college, talk about their work, and see something of the college in action. This can include talking to students in training, which is always a useful source of information, coming, as it were, from the studio floor. Some colleges also hold 'open days' but more significantly all colleges put on annual exhibitions (usually in June and early July) of student's work. When art students complete their courses they mount degree or diploma shows which are all open to the public—these should not be missed—though a telephone call to the college may be necessary to obtain details.

Probably more important than finding out about college work however is the need for you to develop a strong personal interest in the many diverse aspects of art and design. Artists and designers, as creative people, need to have a lively interest in the world around them. One of the functions of artists is to be sensitively aware of the world we live in, to observe it sharply, to comment on it, and respond to what is going on. You therefore need to be alert to your surroundings—not just the visual appearance of our towns and countryside but have a deep knowledge of designed and made objects.

The world of fashion and designed objects, to say nothing of natural form, architecture and landscape, is all around us and designers and craftsmen must be aware of what has been produced in the past and what is being manufactured now.

We can find out a great deal by simply being observant, using our eyes and even drawing or photographing what we see and what interests us. Interesting things are all around us, for example, magazines on the arts and design are readily available and you should, through your public library, become familiar with these. Even non-specialist popular magazines tell us a great deal about the arts, fashion, design and the crafts and what is being produced for the consumer market. In addition to magazines and books, museums and galleries in most towns will help us explore our past traditions in art and learn something of current practice. Even

Before you go to art school

local craft and high street shops can frequently help us see what is going on in the world of fashion and manufactured goods.

So reading, looking and visiting galleries and museums should form a logical preparation. You should not need to be told to look at magazines or visit museums—you should do so because you want to; without this type of self-motivation your chances of success in art and design begin to look less bright.

The mass media, through television, radio and colour magazines, presents us with a large amount of material related to the visual world and our education can start before we go to college if we will only look in a lively and enquiring way. Similarly, interests in the cinema, music, theatre and other arts can all help in building up an attitude of concern and interest in the extensive world of art and design.

At an interview you may well be asked what you really know about your stated field of interest. It's not particularly logical to express an interest in, for example, furniture design, by saying you want to be a 'furniture designer' and then not knowing anything at all about current designers or famous designers of the past, or what's in the shops at the moment.

Not only can we look and read but we can also collect and start to build up sketchbooks, visual notebooks or 'scrapbooks' where we can keep pictures of the things that interest us. Interests can develop into knowledge in this way, and there is so much printed visual material available that it is not difficult to start such a collection, including your own photographs. Artists need to build up a visual reference bank and it is never too early to start.

Finally, it may also help to remember that many courses also include an element of art and design history and complementary studies. Background preliminary reading, or the collection of pictorial material, can be very helpful in starting to develop an interest in this field and beginning to understand something of the history and traditions of art and design and the cultural and social context in which it operates.

3 College studies

1 Introduction – the national picture

Most people, no doubt, find the whole education system bewildering, but none of it is quite so bewildering as higher education in art and design. The range and variety of courses is a complicated maze and finding a clear route requires some help and careful study.

We have relatively more art and design courses in the UK than any other country in the world and selecting one can be a nightmare. The situation is confused—not only are there a large number of courses (more than 300 colleges offer courses in art and design) but there are many different types and levels of course. To make matters even more difficult, courses are not uniform in style, content, or indeed quality.

A further difficulty is that the national organisation and validation of many non-degree courses is currently being changed. In fact the entire non-degree sector is being reorganised under the auspices of the Technician Education Council. Art and Design education has traditionally been susceptible to frequent change—it is a type of education which needs to respond to changing cultural and industrial demands, with new forms of training and new courses, constantly under consideration. This chapter therefore sets out to plot a path through the maze of college based study.

Historically, it has always been difficult to fit art and design education neatly into the mainstreams of advanced higher education. It has, in general, not found a place in the traditional academic corridors of the university nor has it quite been at home within technical education. Art schools, departments and faculties of art have therefore found homes in a variety of places, making a very complicated picture for the school leaver to sort out.

We need first to recall that basically all training for work in art and design is full-time and college based. There is some limited direct-trade training, with part-time attendance at a college, but professional or 'specialist' training is normally full-time, though some of the new DATEC courses can be studied on a part-time basis.

There is a difference of course between professional or vocational training on one hand and recreational studies and general courses related to art and design on the other. Recreational studies are not related to careers and although many

College studies

part-time classes exist throughout the country to provide leisure and art activities, they in no way set out to train or prepare students for work in the profession.

This leaves us with two broad categories—'specialist' or vocational courses and 'general' or combined art and design courses. Specialist courses aim to train students in the professional practice of a specific discipline, to a high creative and technical standard. There are, in simple terms, courses 'in' art and design where skills and talents are developed by practical study into single subject disciplines, leading to a specific employment field. Whereas general art and design courses are usually more concerned with learning 'about' art and its relationship with society and other subjects, rather than the professional practice of skills. Clearly such general courses have a wide academic and educational scope but are less related to employment in the commercial world of art and design. The majority of courses in art and design education are however in vocational and professional study and the emphasis in this section is therefore concerned with courses of this nature.

Degrees and diplomas
In the vocational or professional zone there are two categories of courses—degrees and diplomas. Labels and names get confusing and we sometimes hear the two types of courses referred to as 'degree courses' and 'vocational courses' when in fact both degrees and diplomas are vocational in that they prepare students for a specific career or vocation.

The difference between degrees, on one hand, and diplomas and certificates on the other are not always easily apparent and the standard of practical design work achieved is sometimes very similar.

The main differences, in very simple terms, are that diplomas, certificates or vocational courses may usually be started at an earlier age than that required for degree study, GCE entry requirements are usually less demanding, and some courses of study are of shorter duration. The main difference however is probably found in the scope of courses; with degree study setting out to place the particular discipline in a broader context, while diploma and certificate courses tend to aim at a more narrow, single discipline approach, related to not only a specific industry but very often a particular aspect of that industry, though the new DATEC higher diplomas are, however, generally quite broad in content.

College studies

Who validates the courses? CNAA, DATEC, the universities and colleges

In sorting out our maze of courses one helpful guide is to remember who validates each type of course. By 'validate' we mean who awards the diplomas, certificates or degrees, and who is responsible for the standard of the course.

The Council for National Academic Awards (CNAA) is responsible for the validation of all specialist professional degree courses, awarding in most cases the Council's BA (Hons) degree. As a national body the Council is able to oversee the standard of courses and ensure that appropriate levels of training are provided wherever the courses are taught.

Unlike the so-called degree sector, all vocational diplomas and certificates were, until recently, awarded by the college or school offering the course. However, starting in 1982 many vocational courses are being validated nationally by the Design and Art section of the Technician Education Council (DATEC). This is an on-going process and the vocational sector of art and design is therefore, at present, made up of a mixture of diplomas and certificates; some awarded and validated by DATEC and some still awarded by the college or school that you attend.

The structure is therefore gradually being tidied up, moving towards a simple two part provision with CNAA degrees on one side and DATEC diplomas and certificates on the other. However, the move towards national validation by DATEC is a long and slow process and the existing wide variety is likely to continue for some years yet.

In the specialist area of training we therefore, at present, have two types of training—degree courses, BA (Hons) validated by CNAA, and vocational courses—(i) diplomas and certificates awarded by DATEC and (ii) college diplomas and certificates.

Outside the courses covered in this simple summary are the university courses. Most of the courses offered and validated by the universities are in the more general field of study in art and design. Nearly all specialist professional training in art and design is undertaken by the public sector of higher education (polytechnics, colleges of higher education, colleges and schools of art). There are a few examples where professional training in the practice of art and design is offered as part of a university course, but studies in art and design within the universities is generally of an academic or theoretical nature concerned more with the history of art and its relationship with other subjects. Where practical work, and personal development as an artist, is undertaken in universities, it is usually limited to studies in fine art and often then as part of a combined degree with another subject.

College studies

Art and design workshops and studios do not in general feature within the university provision (except in faculties of engineering) and actually to train as a practising artist, designer or craftsman you would normally therefore need to attend a school or faculty of art. In practice, divisions are not always as clear cut as this. Many new and different courses are springing up and overlaps in approach, between specialist training and general courses, do frequently occur.

Some of the choices to be made

Once you have decided that you are going to pursue a career in art and design you have to decide what type of course you wish to follow. You also may have to choose which art school or college to attend. You may even wish to consider cutting out art school altogether and going straight to work in a commercial studio, drawing office or workshop.

Although provision for direct-trade training is not extensive some limited opportunities do exist. This form of industrial training is only eligible in a limited number of trades and will be discussed more fully under section 4 of this chapter. However, you need to remember that most direct-trade entry training is normally eligible only for young school leavers aged 15 or 16, and although you have the advantage of actually starting, as it were, with a job on the shop floor inside industry, future prospects are tied very much to that single industry or narrow aspect of work.

The more common decision confronting the school leaver is the choice between training on a specialist degree or diploma course or a university course.

We have already described the broad differences between these two types of training so it will largely depend on your talent and aptitude. In general, if you have a genuine and strong talent for art and design, together with all the qualities needed for making things and expressing ideas, then the specialist college of art courses are for you. Put another way, if you actually want to be a practising artist or professional designer then the specialist courses are usually the best, and often only, form of training.

If, however, your practical ability and commitment are less pronounced, with your academic interests more diversely spread—then the broader university course may well be more appropriate. Single minded commitment, with an almost obsessive interest in art, is necessary for a creative professional career whereas a more objective interest in the world of art, and its relationship to history and our cultural traditions, along with other subjects may suggest a university course.

University courses usually require higher academic qualifications

College studies

while art schools require a much higher standard of work in a portfolio, in fact many university courses have no practical component and do not require a folder of work as part of the entry requirement.

Choosing between a degree course and a diploma course is another problem. Sometimes this can be postponed by the school leaver first undertaking a Foundation course (which can lead to further study on a degree or diploma course) or one of the new DATEC diploma courses (after which transfer to a degree course or a higher diploma may be possible). But sometimes the decision has to be made while still at school. Art teachers and local art schools can help in making the decision but, as we see later in this chapter, there are some broad guidelines which may help. For example, Diplomas and Certificates are generally orientated to a single aspect of industry, so this type of course may be appropriate if you are one of those people who actually, at an early stage, really knows without doubt what you want to do. In some cases diploma or certificate courses do tend to focus in one facet of industry and such concentration is fine if you are sure it's right for you.

Diploma and certificate courses may take pupils at an earlier age, and with a lower GCE entry requirement, than degree courses. There is not always much to choose from between high level diplomas and degrees, in terms of the quality of work produced. The main choice may therefore depend on whether you wish to study the specialist subject in the broader, more flexible climate of the degree course or the slightly narrower vocational emphasis of the diploma course. Academic qualificaitons, and other subject interests may influence your decision and it should also be remembered that post-graduate and further advanced study is normally more readily available to graduates than to students possessing diplomas or certificates.

Choosing a college will not be difficult if you intend doing a Foundation course for you will be required to attend your local college, and have no choice. The discretionary nature of grants, available to students on courses below the age of eighteen, usually means that you have to attend initial courses at colleges within your local authority. However, if you choose a university or diploma course you may have to select a course on a national basis.

If you are, while still at school, required to make a choice of art college (though this is normally rare) then it is important to discuss this carefully with your art teacher and not only obtain all possible information, but ideally visit the colleges concerned.

College studies
2 The nature of 'art school' work

When we use the term 'art school' we mean all specialist study in art and design that can be undertaken in faculties of art and design, in polytechnics, departments in colleges of higher education, and schools and colleges of art. Specialist work in art and design goes on in all these places—and other types of institutions as well. Most of the larger colleges of art were absorbed into polytechnics during the 1970s, forming the faculties of art and design in these large multi-disciplinary institutions. This clearly has some advantages but equally the schools and colleges, which operate independently, and the departments in colleges of higher education all offer the same high level of training and resources. In other words a CNAA degree, or a DATEC diploma is of exactly the same value and merit wherever it happens to be taught—so don't be put off going to a smaller art college or a large polytechnic faculty—if you can, have a look at both and decide which offers the course that best suits your particular interests and needs.

Professional specialist training, leading towards working in art and design, is fundamentally concerned with developing your creative, visual and practical skills and is different from other forms of study. Rather than sitting in lecture rooms or studying in the classrooms most of the learning takes place in the studios and workshops. Practical study—or what is nicely termed 'practical scholarship' (just to stress that working with your hands can be as intellectually demanding as any other work) is an active business—it's not a passive process of learning but one in which we learn by actual work experience. Specialist courses can be described as study 'in' art rather than 'about' art—by this we mean that we do not sit and 'learn about art' but we actually make it. The young artist or designer is not only primarily engaged in practical experiment and exploration but he or she must also work in the world of ideas. Eventually, it is not only a case of reacting to study projects set by tutors, but of developing your own ideas in solving problems, and eventually working on your own ideas, rather than an idea or problem given by someone else.

The process of developing your own ideas, or more importantly initiating your own work, can be very demanding. Students sometimes get the idea that they are left too much to their own devices; they may feel lost, possibly wishing to be told what to do. Designers and artists however have to develop and create their own ideas, and make personal responses to problems. The necessary individual and personal development can only occur if the student can build up his own working momentum. Obviously

College studies

tutors and technical experts are there to help and advise you but the capacity for self-initiated work is vital, and this will be one of the qualities looked for at any selection interview.

The majority of work in art schools is therefore actually concerned with solving practical problems, working in studios and workshops and following the design process through to the making of finished products; while at the same time developing your personal ability as a creative individual.

In addition to the world of creative personal ideas, you also need to learn techniques and skills and obtain a thorough working knowledge of materials, machines and processes. Although designers have to learn to work with other people involved in the production process, they also have to get accustomed to working on their own. Design students must therefore be prepared to identify problems to be solved, establish work objectives and plan their own work schedules. This emphasis on working on your own can at times be difficult for the art student in training and require a strong sense of personal motivation.

Art history and complementary studies
While most of your study time is spent in practical work some 15-20% of your course, on degrees and some diplomas, is spent in the study of art and design history together with related and historical studies. Such supporting studies may take many forms. Art and design history is always the predominant related study but other work may include complementary studies relating art to broader social, cultural and economic issues and exploring other related arts, like the cinema, theatre, literature and music. You may in addition find yourself involved in business and management studies, related to your chosen specialist area.

All such related studies work is intended to help put your main practical study into a broader historic and social context—in fact such work is sometimes referred to as 'contextual' studies and clearly forms a very important and demanding aspect of your professional training.

In the same way that the style of study in art schools is somewhat different to other forms of higher education, so the assessment systems are unique to this form of training. Rather than sit formal written examinations, which would be clearly inappropriate, students are assessed by presenting the actual evidence of their practical study. This normally takes the form of an exhibition at which a student displays his work, such assessments are often referred to as 'degree or diploma shows'. Work is however not only submitted for assessment at the end of the course, it is also exhibited and continuously assessed at regular

College studies

intervals.

Assessment in art history and complementary studies varies from college to college. The most common practice is for students to submit essays and other written work throughout the course and then in the final year a thesis on a chosen subject has to be written and submitted for assessment.

Art students not only have to develop their own individual, and very personal skills and abilities, but must also develop a thorough knowledge of current professional practice. This should include not only an awareness of what is going on in the world of art and design, related to their studies, but also should include some realistic experience of production work and industrial conditions. This aspect of training is usually achieved in three ways.

(i) Regular visits to industry and design studios, combined with visits to college from industrial specialists.

(ii) Periods of work in industry and design studios during training. This is sometimes dealt with informally but some courses have a specific period of industrial placement as a formal part of the course. Such courses are normally known as 'sandwich' courses, reflecting the idea that a period of work experience is 'sandwiched' between two periods of college based study.

(iii) A third way of ensuring a thorough contact with current practice is by students coming into contact with working designers, artists and craftsmen. This is achieved on many courses, especially those in the London area, by employing part-time tutors. Part-time tutors are usually artists or designers with current industrial or working experience, who leave their own work for a day or two a week to teach young designers. This contact with practising part-time tutors is a particularly useful way of keeping students in touch with the reality of professional practice.

3 The broad areas of study and specialisation

For many years specialist study in colleges of art, whether at degree level or at diploma or certificate level, has been divided into four main areas—Fine Art, Graphic Art, Textiles/Fashion and Three-Dimensional Design. These broad headings or categories are helpful in that they act as convenient umbrellas under which we can cluster associated disciplines and courses.

One of the confusing and gently irritating things about art and design is the language used to describe activities. The labels frequently need explaining and we have to be sure that we understand what for example we mean by Graphic Design or

College studies

Communication Studies. The four main headings therefore provide a useful guide in classifying and grouping different areas of study leading to professional employment.

Titles and labels tend, like courses, to get out of date. New disciplines and courses are constantly being introduced but in general we can still manage to put them under one of our umbrellas. As an aside it should however be stressed that new types of courses, and groupings of specialisations, do frequently occur and current publications, or your local art college, should be contacted for updated information. In detail the four main headings cover work in the following areas.

Fine Art

Fine art is that activity concerned with the training of artists and sculptors. Courses include the traditional activities of painting, sculpture, drawing and printmaking (etching, lithography, engraving and silk-screen) and also normally offer a wide choice of other media including film, video, and work in photography. Fine art is primarily concerned with offering individual students, with ambition and ability, the opportunity to develop their own expressive and creative ideas in whatever materials and processes are appropriate and available. Fine art is, by its very nature, open ended and explorative. Activities are therefore not prescribed or rigidly structured. Fine art offers a training which has an intrinsic value in itself, irrespective of any vocational outlet. Courses are aimed more at personal development than specific employment areas. A certain amount of training in fine art is considered, by many people, to be fundamental to all work in art and design and many design courses include fine art elements. Fine art is a broad based activity and painters, sculptors, and printmakers are quite commonly employed in other fields of design work and the arts.

Graphic Design

Graphic design is the heading normally used to describe work related to the visual communications industry. It is a large field of study feeding a complicated and diverse industry and is concerned with conveying information or ideas visually, through printing or any other media. Work in graphics is about finding the most efficient ways of communicating ideas and information with words and images; combining the verbal message with the visual presentation.

Graphic design is closely associated with the printing, advertising, publishing and communication industries and the

College studies

activities covered range from technical illustration and typography on one hand to personal illustrative work and film animation on the other. If we think of all the things we use and see, which are printed, or use words and images, then we get some idea of the scope of this area—from the packages and wrapping around the goods we buy to the magazines we read, the road signs that direct us and the television advertisements we watch—all this and much more is 'graphic design'. The term 'commercial art' was at one time used to describe some of this work but the phrase no longer covers the necessary range and 'graphic design' or 'communication studies' are the terms now in use.

Courses and work in graphic design can therefore cover any of the following activities—scientific, medical and technical illustration, book and magazine illustration, lettering and typography, book design, editorial design, package design, all fields of advertising and publicity design, aspects of printing and publishing, photography, film making and film animation, television graphics together with work in video and computers.

Our industrial and commercial society increasingly requires the services of graphic designers for clear and effective visual communication, in all manner of fields, and there are a great variety of courses, and job outlets. In graphic design the artist works within the technology of the communication industry, from printing to the computer, to produce the graphic images we see all around us.

Textiles/Fashion

Textiles/Fashion is a rather misguiding title—though we still persist in using it. The heading broadly covers that work concerned with the design of all the clothes we wear and the design and production of all the materials we use to make these clothes.

But textiles as a label is not limited to the materials we use for clothing but includes all the many woven or printed fabrics that we use in our homes and at work. These range from curtains and furnishing fabrics to wall papers, floor coverings, carpets, plastic tiles and surfaces. Another widely used term for textile design is 'decorative surfaces', and such a label can better describe the very wide range of designed surfaces and materials that surround us. Textiles as a word suggests woven or printed fabrics, while many surfaces are constructed or produced in different ways. In addition to industrially produced surfaces the craft areas of weaving, embroidery and knitting also come within this category, along with their industrial applications.

College studies

The fashion industry, and related courses, are wider in scope and variety than the 'high' fashion of expensive *'haute couture'*. Fashion as an activity covers the design of all clothing from high street clothes to boutique dresses and includes industrial protective clothing, uniforms and theatrical costumes, sports and leisure wear, and also children's and men's wear. Fashion as a subject also embraces the extensive field of clothing accessories—including lingeries, millinery, shoe design, handbags, scarves and gloves—in fact all the many things we dress up in.

Three-Dimensional Design

Three-dimensional design is intended to describe the extremely wide range of products that in simple terms have three-dimensional form—in other words, solid objects rather than flat two-dimensional work.

The various industries, and range of courses in this area, are as extensive as are all the objects and things around us which we use every day. The scale of activities can be described in a number of ways. We can, for instance, think of all the materials in which goods are produced, from glass and plastic to wood and metal, or alternatively we can consider the range from small craft made objects, such as jewellery and ceramics, to large industrial design or engineering products, such as machinery and vehicles. As with other areas of work, traditional hand craft activities are found alongside industrial mass production. We therefore have to consider the craft industries together with industrial consumer products—which can include anything from electric irons and fountain pens to telephones and chairs. The areas of study are usually listed as ceramics, glass, furniture, jewellery, silver, plastics, and other metals, together with all industrial and product design including aspects of engineering design.

In addition to the design of all products we use; three-dimensional design, as an umbrella phrase, also includes the extensive fields of interior design and theatre design. Interior design comprises the design of the interiors of buildings including anything from homes to hospitals and factories to luxury yachts—in fact any interior space we use to work or live in—even buses and tube trains. Interior design also incorporates the major field of exhibition and display design. Theatre design includes the training of the designer for the theatre, cinema and television, which is an area which makes a heavy demand for set and 'prop' designs.

Three-dimensional design may therefore be described as covering the training of the designer-craftsman for the traditional

College studies

industrial crafts, together with the industrial designer, engineering designer (sometimes known as product designer) and interior and theatre designer.

Engineering Design

The breadth of subjects coming under the heading of three-dimensional design is so extensive that it cannot all be contained within art school training. For example, although interior design is closely associated with architecture, the professional training of architects takes place in separate schools, or departments of architecture. Similarly, the training of engineering designers largely takes place outside colleges of art and design. Studies in three-dimensional design, in art colleges, spreads as far as courses in industrial design (engineering).

Industrial design (engineering) covers the appearance, and users requirements, of things such as refrigerators, radios, washing machines, vehicles, and medical and scientific equipment. Larger scale work, and technological design, is about the design of the operating function, rather than the outward visual appearance, and this is the responsibility of the engineering designer. This includes, for example, electrical and electronic engineering design, mechanical engineering design, and civil, marine, aeronautical and production engineering design. To train for these fields you either need first to get an engineering degree or to combine an industrial apprenticeship with college attendance.

To summarise, the industrial designer is primarily concerned with the appearance of products, and the way people use them, while the engineering designer is mainly concerned with a product's performance and production.

4 The courses – their scope and content

The courses in this section have been broadly divided into the two basic categories—*specialist* and *general*. The first category includes those courses with a specific vocational and professional objective. The second group covers those more general courses, which do not lead primarily to professional practice as a working designer, artist or craftsman.

It should be stressed, at this stage, that the pattern of courses change from time to time. New courses and modifications are constantly being introduced and it is therefore important always to check either with local colleges, or with career or art teachers. It is also necessary to confirm that information in any leaflet or publication is up to date.

College studies
Specialist courses

(i) Foundation studies
While direct entry from sixth form is possible, in exceptional cases, to degree courses (see section 5 'Entry qualifications') the CNAA's preferred route to specialist degree courses is through a foundation course. Some foundation studies are now subsumed into DATEC diplomas, but the principle of a preliminary pre-degree period, remains the same.

As we have already seen foundation courses are an essential part of the training of the artist, bridging the gap between school and specialist degree study. The enormous expansion of art and design activities, and the wide range of specialist skills demanded, obviously cannot be matched or accommodated in school work and many schools are unable to extend their art and design coverage beyond general drawing, painting and limited craft activities; though recent developments in design education are helping to extend secondary school work. School leavers cannot therefore be reasonably expected to assess their aptitude for specific specialist training on the basis of such general experience. Specialist degree courses are not multi-disciplinary with built in mobility from one specialist discipline to another—so when you've chosen your course you have to be sure it's the right one for you. Hence the need for foundation courses which normally occupy one year between leaving school and entering a degree course—though a few two-year foundation courses may still be found.

Foundation courses are intended to offer a broad introduction to industrial design as well as fine art and can help students to develop the necessary talent, and decide in which particular area their interests and abilities lie. Courses set out to provide students with a sound foundation in visual and practical study and to develop the basic process of visual analysis and observation. You will encounter a wide range of materials and experiences designed primarily to develop your own potential and acquaint you with the underlying problems common to the professional artist and designer in the field. An even more important function of foundation work is however to help you diagnose the future specialist direction for which you are best suited; and having done so, help you select the college whose course is most likely to be appropriate to your specific needs.

Application to foundation courses is through your local college. Under present grant awarding arrangements courses do not attract mandatory awards and the discretionary award for foundation studies requires that students are home based and attend the

College studies

college within their local authority.

Foundation courses contribute significantly to higher education in that they offer a unique opportunity for personal development and decision making. A career decision taken after a year's exploratory study is more likely to be a meaningful and accurate choice than a random decision taken after possibly a single interview. This is no doubt reflected in the subsequently extremely low drop out rate—from specialist degree courses following foundation studies. However beware, even on a year's course, time is short, and if you are preparing for entry to degree or vocational courses in the following year, you may have to decide on your specialisation at the end of the first term or early in the spring term; to give you time to prepare relevant work for a degree course interview.

Final specialist career or degree course decisions are usually best left until you are actually working on a foundation course. In fact an open minded attitude is probably advisable, as you cannot know where your real aptitude may lie until you have some experience of the whole range of choices. As you cannot enter a degree course until you are 18 years of age the earliest you can start a one-year course is at 17—though many students wait until they have completed their sixth form studies. On the completion of a foundation course the majority of students apply for places on the CNAA specialist degree courses but some may move onto other courses in art and design, including for example combined degrees and DATEC higher diplomas. It should be stressed that on completion of a foundation course a further formal application has to be made, which will not necessarily be in the same institution. A foundation course is not intended necessarily to prepare students for degree courses within the same college, but to find an appropriate place for further specialist study wherever it may be available in the country.

Foundation courses throughout the country are listed in *Design Courses in Great Britain* published by the Design Council (see Bibliography page 143) but careers officers, art teachers, libraries or local art colleges can give you details of your nearest college. In addition the Regional Advisory Councils for Further Education produce regional guides to courses. See pages 148-49.

(ii) Specialist CNAA degree courses
Fine Art, Graphic Design, Textiles/Fashion, Three-Dimensional Design
As we have seen, very few university courses include provision for professional art and design studio or workshop practice. The graduate training of artists and designers is therefore almost

exclusively supervised by the Council for National Academic Awards. The Council is the largest single degree awarding body in the United Kingdom and encourages colleges, whenever appropriate, to suit their courses to the needs of industry, commerce and the professions. This approach provides the extra dimension of industrial or professional practice to the courses, further distinguishing them from the university sector.

CNAA specialist degrees are therefore primarily aimed at professional work outlets in art and design. To meet these objectives courses need to be highly specialised, largely full-time, and single discipline. In other words to obtain employment and sell your skills in a competitive market you need highly skilled specialists rather than people with general mediocre ability over a broad field. This is possibly stating the case too strongly but if courses are to be vocational then we must recognise that, in a competitive and difficult world, specialist excellence is more marketable, in most areas of industry, than broad general levels of achievement—however desirable breadth and diversity may appear.

CNAA BA (Hons) specialist degrees cover a wide range of study disciplines which are offered under the four main areas of fine art, graphic design, textiles/fashion and three-dimensional design. Of the four main groupings fine art is clearly the one area not related to work in the design profession. Though the basic fine art skills of painting, drawing and visual analysis are common underlying elements of design training. While the majority of CNAA specialist courses are concerned with a single subject specialisation a small number, in particular fields, are multi-disciplinary and are referred to in section (vi).

Study on specialist courses is mainly practical, concentrating on both your general developments as an artist/designer, and on the special skills and techniques associated with your chief area of study. Studio and workshop practice is related both to your personal development and the needs of industry and the profession. The nature of specialisation varies from course to course, and with individual needs. Some courses may keep you narrowly to one discipline, while other courses offer a range of options within a single area; though students tend to move gradually towards identifying a narrow field of interest as the course progresses. Sometimes these two approaches may distinguish degrees from diplomas—with degree courses offering the whole range of associated specialisms while diplomas may concentrate on a single strand. In general, however, courses tend logically to encourage individual specialisation towards the end of the course; though as the world of industry becomes more

College studies

complex further specialisation is often pushed into post-graduate work.

In addition to the emphasis on practical studies, degree courses also contain an element of art history and complementary studies, usually between 15 and 20% of your time. These studies set out to provide a broad historical, social, cultural and theoretical context to practical work. Sometimes these studies are specifically related to your main degree subject, and may include relevant business and management studies and the history of your chief design area. Alternatively, supporting studies may be used to broaden and complement narrowly concentrated practical studies. Supporting theoretical studies, and the history of art and design are built into all degree courses, and students are normally required to attend lectures, write essays and present a final thesis on a selected topic. Ability to cope with this theoretical component, and benefit from it, is a factor to be considered when choosing a degree course rather than a certificate or college diploma course, which normally would not include such a significant amount of theoretical work.

Most degree courses require three years full-time study, with a minimum entry of 18, normally preceded by a one-year foundation course (though a few isolated courses are beginning to consider some form of part-time attendance). Some of the specialist courses are however organised on a sandwich basis, in which case they are four years in duration. These four year full-time courses are designed to give students experience of working in industry during their course of study. All degree courses, three and four year (except fine art), set out to give students experience in industry. While the three year courses may do this in an informal way the four year sandwich courses build it in as a fixed requirement. The period of practical training in the relevant industry or profession may consist of a whole year, usually the third, and this is often described as a 'thick' sandwich. Alternatively shorter periods, totalling six months or less, are described as 'thin' sandwich courses. Whatever the length of industrial placement the object is the same—to give the student a supervised, but realistic, mid course industrial experience during which real world practise can be compared and related to theory. During the placement in industry your student grant is normally suspended and you are paid by the company or firm employing you. Sandwich courses, in a sense, bridge the traditional gap between learning on the job (apprenticeships) and learning away from work in college.

Detailed information on all CNAA courses is contained in the Council's publication *A Directory of First Degree and Diploma*

College studies of Higher Education Courses (available from CNAA at 344/354 Gray's Inn Road, London, WC1X 8BP. The Careers Research Advisory Centre (CRAC) also publishes a comprehensive *Degree Course Guide* and the Design Council's *Design Courses in Britain* contains all necessary information on design courses (not including fine art). *Which Degree* published annually by Haymarket Publishing Limited, also gives brief summaries of Art and Design degree courses. Refer to the bibliography on page 143 for further details.

(iii) DATEC diplomas and certificates
Vocational, non-degree courses in art and design, are at present undergoing reorganisation. Outside the degree sector, in advanced art and design education, there have always been a large number of colleges offering vocational diplomas and certificates. The range and quality of these college diplomas has varied widely, depending on the college making the award.

In an effort to unify this complicated system of college validated courses, and following a Government report, the Technician Education Council (TEC) set up in 1977 a committee for art and design—now generally known as DATEC. DATEC's job was to unify the system of non-degree courses in art and design and establish a nationwide standard of course approval, validation and awards—exactly parallel to the role of CNAA for the degree sector.

A further aim of the national validation by DATEC is to ensure that students should be able to progress from DATEC courses to degree and post-graduate courses. The CNAA has, in fact, recently accepted such qualifications for purposes of admission to first degree and diploma of higher education courses. DATEC, as part of the Technician Education Council, is therefore responsible for a new national system of vocational non-degree courses in art and design. DATEC courses began to be introduced from September 1980—but it is a gradual process or reorganisation, with much work still to be done during the transition towards a unified national system. Courses will remain richly varied, reflecting the local needs and college strengths, but the level and standard of work will be consistent throughout the system. During the changeover there will no doubt be some confusion, as with any new system, and college awarded diplomas and certificates will no doubt continue to run alongside DATEC courses.

There are four main TEC awards—Certificate, Diploma, Higher Certificate and Higher Diploma. The study arrangements for DATEC courses are therefore structured within a system of certificates and diplomas together with higher certificates and

College studies

higher diplomas. All awards may be achieved by any mode of study—full-time, part-time, sandwich and block release, though there will be many regional and college variations—so a visit to your local college is essential.

> In broad terms the courses are as follows:
> Certificate—normally three years part-time or two years full-time—entry age 16 or more, with at least three CSEs (grade III).
> Diploma—normally two years full-time or two/three years sandwich study—entry age of 16 or more, three 'O' levels normally minimum requirement.
> Higher Certificate/Higher Diploma—minimum entry age 18 or more together with a DATEC art and design certificate or diploma.

You may be able to enter a higher certificate or higher diploma if you have suitable GCE 'O' levels and/or 'A' levels, or from an art and design foundation course. Higher certificates are normally two years part-time or one-year full-time. Higher diplomas are normally two years full-time or two/three years sandwich study. There are a number of differences between certificates/higher certificates and diplomas/higher diplomas. Certificates require less academic entry qualifications but more significantly they aim generally at a single specific study with in-depth specialisation—in other words they are narrower in approach. Certificates normally also place more emphasis on practical skills with materials and processes and may be more predominantly part-time, or suited for block release from industry; in addition they are generally intended to be identified with local industry and employment needs.

Diplomas on the other hand are more likely to involve broader subject categories, with groups of specialist subjects seen in a wider context. Work on diplomas is usually more analytical with creative design work related to other knowledge. Diplomas are more frequently full-time (or sandwich) and more likely to be identified with regional and national industrial needs.

DATEC courses are offered under three main headings—Graphics, Textiles/Fashion and Three-Dimensional Design. Unlike CNAA degrees DATEC does not cover the fourth area, Fine Art, for the obvious reason that DATEC, as part of the Technician Education Council, is clearly responsible for training leading to employment in the design industry.

However, in addition to the three categories DATEC also offers general art and design courses. There are basically two categories of general courses. The first includes certificates and diplomas in general vocational design, designed to give an introduction to a wide range of design studies. The second category covers general diploma courses in art and design devised to prepare students for entry to an advanced course of specialist study. This could be either a TEC higher award or a degree course in art and design. General diplomas are very similar to foundation courses and are specifically designed to help students choose the area of further study which suits them best. In fact, many foundation courses have been merged into general DATEC diploma courses, providing the same type of diagnostic training, which can lead to either entry onto a degree course or a TEC higher diploma. The possible movement across from certificates to diplomas or from diplomas to degree courses is one of the interesting possibilities that DATEC courses present.

Although DATEC is a comparatively new organisation it is worth remembering that the courses are being offered by long established colleges, thoroughly experienced in training artists and designers, and in offering courses. Don't be put off just because they are new courses—in fact that may be a good reason for considering them. The courses are planned in close association with industry, and are strongly vocational in essence, offering a very viable alternative to degree level work, while at the same time allowing for transfer to degree courses if appropriate.

Further details about DATEC courses can be obtained from your local college or from the Technician Education Council, 76 Portland Place, London, W1N 4AA.

(iv) College diplomas and certificates and professional qualifications
While vocational non-degree course in art and design are being reorganised a confusing variety of courses may well remain. The general movement is towards the non-degree sector of diplomas and certificates being nationally validated by DATEC. But local certificates and diplomas, awarded and validated by individual colleges, will continue as a further alternative study route for a number of years. The ultimate aim is to establish a simple two-part system for advanced study in art and design—the degree sector (largely validated by CNAA) and the diploma/certificate sector (validated by DATEC). However the process of rationalisation towards this will take time—during which college validated courses will continue.

Vocational courses in art and design (as non-degree courses are often called) provide professional and practical training in art and design, as opposed to the broader academic approach of degree

College studies

courses and higher diplomas. Most vocational students attend courses in their own area (except for high level diplomas) since few local authorities will provide grants for students for vocational study outside their locality—whereas degree students are eligible for a mandatory grant wherever they choose to study.

The content, duration and entry requirements for college diplomas and certificates are not standardised but vary from college to college and it is impossible therefore to describe them accurately. In general they set out to provide a professional vocational training in practical skills and train students to a high level of proficiency. As well as providing a training for designers, related to specific industries, vocational courses also meet the demand for craft and design technicians. The design industry requires skilled craftsmen to work with creative designers. This work often includes such professional skills as model making, technical graphics and draughtmanship, and aspects of, for example, technical photography. Vocational courses prepare students for this work.

College validated vocational courses vary widely in terms of length of study from one to three and sometimes four years, and it is necessary to check individual entry requirements and course content before applying. Many of the courses are linked to local needs and industry, but this also varies from area to area and needs to be checked.

Many colleges will continue to offer independent courses while the DATEC reorganisation proceeds. A vocational course at present may therefore lead to a certificate or diploma, awarded by a college or polytechnic, or a regional awards—such as a Southern Regional Diploma. In addition, many diplomas or certificates lead to membership of a professional body or organisation.

Professional qualifications
We have seen how much art and design education aims to train students for particular professional areas of art and design. Many courses, especially those at vocational level, were set up in consultation with industry and the professions, who in many cases approved the course content and aims.

In addition to academic qualifications, practising designers also frequently require a qualification from the professional body related to their field of work. The recognition of the designers professional standing, demonstrated by membership of his or her professional body, is often important in developing a practice or in obtaining commissions.

Some aspects of the design profession consider training as a two part process; one the initial academic qualification, followed

College studies

subsequently by membership to a professional body. Professional qualifications may sometimes only be obtained after working and practising as a designer for a period after leaving college, but the first step towards full professional membership can be taken while at college. It is therefore possible to obtain two qualifications at the end of your course, an academic one and a professional one. The professional qualification may be obtained by taking a special examination or, in some cases, by completing a further year at the end of the course. Alternatively, the qualification may be obtained by completing the course satisfactorily and having your work assessed by representatives of the particular professional body.

Relationships between a college and a particular professional body vary. There is a few for example that professional qualifications should only follow successful professional practice and experience and that college work should not be influenced by the possibly conflicting requirements of a professional body. Some courses, offering a professional qualification, may have entry requirements jointly agreed by the college and the professional association concerned so that entry to the course, or the course qualification, is equivalent to entry to the professional body.

The professional bodies and qualifications generally associated with art and design education are as follows:

The Society of Industrial Artists and Designers—offering Diploma Licenciate membership to students—LSIA/DipSIA.

The Society of Designer Craftsmen—with Licenciate membership—LSDC.

The British Institute of Interior Design—Associate Membership—ABID.

The Institute of Incorporated Photographers.

The British Display Society—BDS.

The Textiles Institute—with associate membership for students—ATI.

The Communication Advertising and Marketing Foundation—CAM.

The main professional membership schemes, associated with art and design courses, are as follows:

College studies

Society of Industrial Artists and Designers (SIAD) — Diploma Membership
The SIAD is the recognised chartered professional association for designers. Diploma membership of the Society, which is a professional rather than academic qualification, is offered as part of many courses. Students taking a course, approved by the Society, may register through their college at the end of the course. Such students must normally hold five 'O' levels and have completed four years full-time study.

Professional Qualifying Examination of the Institute of Incorporated Photographers
This examination is planned to provide broadly based education in photography, including the principles of photography, photographic science, together with business and professional studies.

National Diplomas, Advanced Level of the British Display Society
Two year full-time courses are available leading to National Diplomas, in retail display, exhibition and service display. Courses include elements of lettering, display theory, fashion, graphic design and exhibition design. Entry requirements are normally four GCE's at 'O' level.

British Institute of Interior Design
Associate membership of the BIID may be obtained by students completing a recognised college course in interior design, followed by twelve months professional experience. Technician membership of the BIID may be obtained by students who complete a recognised Design Technicians Course.

Communication Advertising and Marketing Education Foundation
The CAM Creative Diploma is awarded to students who satisfactorily complete a three year Graphic Design course and in addition obtain the CAM certificate (including a project and written papers).

The Textile Institute and The Clothing Institute
These two separate bodies are associated with a number of courses.

The Textile Institute's Associate Examination, which normally forms part of courses in textile technology, leads to associate membership (ATI) and can also be used towards qualifying students as chartered textile technologists.

Some students in clothing and fashion design may begin their training by taking a full-time course, lasting three or four years, leading to the examination of the Clothing Institute. Training includes clothing production, pattern cutting, management, marketing and design.

Professional bodies usually have several levels of membership, ranging from Licentiate and Associate membership (for example LSIA or ASIA) to full member or fellow (MSIA or FSIA). Fellows and full members are naturally very senior forms of membership, awarded usually to designers of experience and high reputation. Professional qualifications, while more normally associated with vocational courses, are also frequently part of the final assessment procedures on degree courses. Many degree courses do give students the option to be assessed for membership to a professional body at the end of their courses.

Finally, it may help in considering the role of professional bodies to distinguish between *education* on one hand and *training* on the other. Education ideally sets out to broaden, develop and 'draw out' individual talents, while training is more concerned with instruction and 'putting in' skills, known facts and techniques. For over a hundred years now the debate between the sometimes conflicting needs of industry, and the academic aims of college based education, has been going on, nowhere so noticeably as in the art schools.

Details of College Diplomas and Certificates may be found in *Design Courses in Britain* published by the Design Council and *Art and Design Education in the Region* published by the Regional Advisory Council for Technological Education for each region of the country. See Bibliography and addresses section for further details. Names and addresses of professional bodies are set out in full on pages 148 to 155.

(v) Engineering design courses and training
The four main headings or groupings of subjects (Fine Art, Graphic Design, Textiles/Fashion, Three-Dimensional Design) stretch as far as including under three-dimensional design, industrial and product design and industrial design (engineering). Art school training in industrial design is predominantly concerned with the appearance of things whereas the engineering designer is responsible for how a machine or piece of equipment actually works. Putting it simply, the art school trained industrial designer looks after the appearance, visual style and users requirements of such items as television sets, telephones or refrigerators, but an engineering designer designs the working inside.

The design of engineering products was, until relatively

College studies

recently, regarded mainly as a technical problem to be handled by engineers and not designers. Industry and the public have however come gradually to realise that appearance and efficiency of handling are equally important functions.

The industrial designer, in addition to understanding visual and functional properties, must also at least understand the engineering problems connected with whatever product he is designing. He is not expected however to have the thorough technological knowledge of a professionally qualified design engineer—that requires a different training. Industrial design (engineering) courses may therefore be followed in faculties of art and design, or colleges of art offering specialist CNAA BA (Hons) courses, but engineering design training is obtained through a separate route.

There are, in simple terms, two ways of training as a design engineer—technician courses and degree courses. Technician courses usually accompany industrial apprenticeships. During the apprenticeship day release or block release attendance would be made to a college or institute of further education to follow a course of study. As a technician you would work with an engineering designer on such things as draughting and the prototype and model building of his design. Careers teachers or officers have details of firms operating technician apprenticeships.

Degree courses in engineering design are usually offered at a polytechnic or university. An engineering designer needs substantial technical knowledge, which takes a long time to acquire, before actual products can be designed. It is necessary therefore to train as an engineer and then specialise as a designer.

Entry to a degree course in engineering design requires a minimum of three 'O' levels and 'A' levels, usually Maths and Physics. Appropriate degree courses are found in polytechnics and the universities particularly those with a technological bias, but a list of engineering courses can be found in the UCCA handbook and the CNAA Directory of First Degree Courses.

(vi) Art teaching

Art teaching, whether in a secondary school, further education or an art college offered, until recently, many career opportunities. Teaching provided sufficient free time for young artists and designers to continue with their own art work and the one-year training, following a degree, was a logical continuation of their art training. Unfortunately, the situation has now changed dramatically. The fall in the national birthrate has drastically reduced the number of children at school and this, combined with recent public expenditure cuts, has lead to a situation where very few jobs in schools are available. Government education cuts have also severely reduced the number of teaching jobs in higher education, particularly affecting the number of part-time teaching posts in art schools, colleges and polytechnic faculties. Practising artists, designers and craftsmen have in the past often looked to part-time teaching for a secure basic regular income. Many, now famous designers and artists, were helped by part-time teaching—which gave them sufficient time to continue their own work, and the necessary security while waiting to establish their reputation, or professional practice. Part-time teaching not only plays an important role in helping the nation's artists and designers get a start in their professional career but, even more importantly, brings students in training at art school into contact with practising designers and artists.

The two routes—BEd and PGCE
Teaching has now become an all graduate profession. The former certificates in education have been discontinued and to teach in general education you now require a degree in education (BEd) or a post-graduate certificate in education. To train as an art teacher you therefore need to either obtain a BEd degree, with art and design as a major subject, or hold a first degree in art and design followed by a one-year post-graduate art teacher qualification—(either the art teachers certificate or diploma (ATC/D) or a post-graduate certificate in education (PGCE).

All courses in initial teacher education include studies in the theory of education, professional studies and periods of school experience. The difference between the BEd route and the post-graduate route of initial training is in the level of involvement with practical studies in art and design. On a BEd course art and design will form a relatively small specialist option. Whereas a student on a PGCE course will have specialised in art for three or four years and theoretical studies in education, and school experience, will be concentrated into the final post-graduate year. The BEd trained art teacher is therefore likely to have a wider general experience of teaching, and will possibly be expected to teach other subjects, whereas the PGCE student will have specialist experience in depth of one subject. Put another way, the BEd student is trained primarily as a teacher (it is after all a degree in education) with art and design seen as an additional option—along with other school subjects—whereas the PGCE route is concerned with professionally trained artists, who then add teaching skills to their previous training.

PGCE courses are only open to graduates. Students following a diploma or vocational course are not eligible for post-graduate art

College studies

teacher training courses. Some applicants from diploma courses may, in exceptional cases, be eligible for shortened BEd courses but normally a student leaving a vocational course would have to complete a full BEd degree in order to enter the teaching profession. It should incidentally be noted that those entering the teaching profession, in any subject, will from 1984 onwards, need GCE passes at 'O' level in English and Mathematics.

The difference between ATC/D courses and the PGCE
A post-graduate certificate in education normally offers a one-year course of training for graduates in all subjects. An art teachers certificate, or diploma, offers a one-year training to art and design graduates only

Art and design may be studied as a main subject on some general PGCE courses. Alternatively, a number of PGCE courses are exclusively designed for the training of specialist art teachers. Art and design graduates who may wish to teach in primary schools, or work as a general subject teacher, in middle or secondary schools, will probably find a general PGCE course more suited to their needs than an ATC/D course, which is aimed at specialist secondary art teaching. Some special PGCE courses also exist for training Craft, Design and Technology teachers while an ATC/D course can be a relevant qualification for work in CDT providing your first degree is related to specialist workshop needs.

Art and craft on the BEd course
The ordinary BEd degree, without honours, includes some art and design studies, but in most cases work is aimed at the primary school level or non-specialist secondary school teaching. Specialist art and design teaching in secondary education would normally be undertaken by a PGCE trained teacher or a BEd student, who had continued to an honours degree, with some emphasis in art.

It must however be noted, with some serious regret, that the amount of time given to practical studies in art and design on most BEd courses is now very small. If you therefore have a real ability in art and craft, and want to teach, select your BEd course very carefully as you may well find opportunities for practical studies limited to a minor option, and submerged by theoretical written studies. This move away from practical studies, in part, has been the price paid for an all graduate teaching profession and it could well have a serious impact on the standard of future art education. If you want to teach and have a talent for art then the specialist PGCE course route may be most suited to you.

Craft, Design and Technology (CDT) and design education

Craft, design and technology is one of the few expanding areas in secondary teaching at present, and one of the few subjects in which there are unfilled posts. In recent years much has been done to promote and establish studies in design education in schools. The importance of design in all our lives, and the need to understand the impact of design decisions in a technological world, has become increasingly important. Design education, aiming, among other things, to relate art and craft with technology is gradually becoming recognised as a central and critical part of our education.

Higher and adult education

Part-time or full-time opportunities in higher, further or adult education are not normally offered to college leavers without further post-graduate study or some years of experience. Teachers and lecturers in art and design are normally appointed on the basis of their professional ability and expertise as artists. In specialist art training the teaching is based on practical work related to professional and commercial needs. It is therefore essential to have teachers who are practising professional artists, designers or craftsmen of some standing and experience. For teaching in art colleges, or faculties and departments of art in higher education, a formal teaching qualification is not necessary (though it may be extremely useful) as teachers are employed primarily on the basis of their knowledge and skill as practising artists.

The CNAA *Directory of First Degree and Diploma of Higher Education Courses* contains details of the Council's courses in Education. A full list of all colleges offering Bachelor of Education courses and post-graduate certificate courses is available from The Central Register and Clearing House, 3 Crawford Place, London, W1H 2BN. This information is also contained in *The Handbook of Colleges and Departments of Education* published by NATFHE by Lund Humphries. Details of Art Teachers' Certificate and Diploma courses are available from the Clearing House for post-graduate Courses in Art Education, The Manor House, Heather, Leicestershire, LE6 1QP.

(vii) Post-graduate study — advanced studies

Post-graduate work in art and design has increased in recent years for a number of reasons. As the world of design and technology becomes more complicated and demanding, and as the range of necessary knowledge becomes wider, so it becomes more necessary to obtain further specialist training after obtaining a

College studies

degree. The so-called 'specialist' first degrees cannot always cover the range of new and expanding knowledge in sufficient depth and students may therefore increasingly need to continue their studies after graduating. In addition, as the world of design technology continues to change so rapidly, many qualified designers may have to return to college, in 'mid-career', for further post-graduate study or refresher courses. Post-graduate study, as well as providing more advanced technological training, can also offer individual students the chance of further personal and academic development.

Post-graduate study falls into two distinct areas—the first extends your art and design training, usually providing an opportunity to develop further a single field already studied at first degree level. The second consists of courses which equip you for entry to special occupations, normally including new disciplines and adding a year of specialist professional trainng to your first degree qualification. Examples of this category would include art teaching, art history, art therapy and courses in arts administration. In the first category there are a large number of full and part-time taught courses, leading to a masters degree (MA), or post-graduate certificate or diploma, normally lasting from one to three years. In addition there are countless opportunities for personal research. Personal research (as opposed to attending a taught course) may lead to an MPhil or PhD qualification—though these at present are predominantly theoretical in nature.

Students are no doubt often attracted to the idea of extending their art education, but there are dangers in taking up post-graduate work purely to put off a decision about future work, or to avoid facing up to the immediate hazards of the job market. Post-graduate work should generally be seen as an opportunity to develop personal skills, and study new technologies in depth, or add a new professional skill as an extension to a degree.

Post-graduate entry requirements are normally the completion of an appropriate first degree at a sufficiently high level. The majority of post-graduate work is open to graduates, though there are some exceptions where higher diplomas or certificates may be acceptable. Many colleges may sometimes offer opportunities for advanced studies where individual workshop or studio based work can be pursued; either leading towards a post-graduate college diploma or certificate, or working on industrially financed research projects. The area of industrial sponsorship for post-graduate research is developing in art and design and, in addition to centres such as the Royal College of Art, many other major colleges offer taught MA courses and also encourage individual research projects; often providing opportunities for

College studies

students to work as a research assistant or research fellow. There are therefore increasing opportunities for post-graduate and advanced studies, depending on how well your talent develops during your first degree course.

Unfortunately, grants for post-graduate work are not readily available for work outside recognised major courses and part-time modes of study, or industrial backing, have frequently to be sought.

(viii) Part-time vocational courses—trade based training
Although the majority of courses leading towards work in the art and design profession are full-time, there are opportunities for part-time study and trade-based training in a limited number of fields. Normally part-time courses of study are linked with the employment in the relevant trade or industry, with the young employee being released from work to attend college on a day, block or evening basis. This method or route of training is usually aimed at the young, early school leaver of 15 or 16 years of age.

Part-time vocational courses, and trade based study, are available for those training in fields such as display, silversmithing, printing, tailoring, millinery, furniture, certain areas within the textiles and clothing industries and other industrial crafts.

Many of these part-time courses lead to the certificate of the City and Guilds of London Institute (CGLI)—while others may lead to diplomas or certificates awarded by colleges, professional bodies or regional organisations. This type of study is normally concerned with training design technicians or industrial craftsmen, rather than industrial designers.

Information on the City and Guilds Certificates and other part-time vocational courses is given in the Regional Advisory Council for Technological Education's *Index of Courses,* available from Tavistock House South, Tavistock Square, London, WC1H 9LR. For details of City and Guilds courses contact the City and Guilds of London Institute, 76 Portland Place, London, W1N 4AA.

General courses
The following groups are 'general' in the sense that they do not set out primarily to train professional designers, in specific vocational areas; but have either a more flexible broad study base, or are concerned with theoretical or contextual studies.

(ix) History of Art
While studies in art history are an integral part of all specialist art and design courses (usually for example comprising some 15% of

College studies

degree study time), the subject can also be studied in its own right. Degrees in the history of art and design are therefore offered at universities and some polytechnics.

If you do not possess the necessary practical skills and talents for training as an artist or designer, but have a strong interest in art, then your interest may lean towards art criticism, history and appreciation. This is not to suggest that theory and practice need to be separated, in fact many art history courses recognise that it helps to have some practical experience, to which historical theory can be related. For example, many students on purely practical courses find they may be more interested in historical studies and go on to study the subject at post-graduate level, with the advantage of having already obtained some useful practical knowlege. Most courses provide the opportunity for students to engage in some practical studio work. This supports the historical studies and provides the historian with some background knowledge of media and techniques. Art historians do not have to be painters, but it clearly helps to have some practical working knowledge, and many courses reflect this by providing access to studios and workshops.

Traditionally, and at most universities, the history of art is concerned with the history of painting, sculpture and architecture, but recent developments, particularly in polytechnic courses, have introduced studies in the history of design, film and cinema. Within the university sector, where most history of art courses are located the courses normally cover the history of painting, sculpture and architecture of Western Europe, from the middle ages to the present century. A few courses deal with the art and architecture of classical antiquity, and some now include the history of film and design.

In general university courses in art history are of three basic kinds—
1 Those that offer a general wide historical survey from, for example, classical antiquity to the present day.
2 Specialist study of a specific historical period.
3 Studies concerned with the ideas underlying art history, such as aesthetics and criticism. Many institutions offer all three approaches in varying combinations and with different emphasis.

Art history courses within polytechnics tend to involve students in more practical work and to offer more opportunities for studying the history of design, film and the modern period. In fact some of the polytechnic based courses in art history could be described as multi-disciplinary in that practical study options may be given substantial weighting. It is important however to distinguish between a first degree in art history, irrespective of how much practical work it may contain, and a multi-disciplinary or combined degree—discussed in the next section.

Full details of art history courses are contained in the Careers Research and Advisory Centre (CRAC) *Degree Course Guide:- Art and Design including Art History*

CNAA courses also appear in the CNAA's *Directory of First Degree and Diploma of Higher Education Courses.*

(x) Combined, multi-disciplinary and general degrees
Combined or multi-disciplinary courses can be placed in two broad categories:

1 Those that combine art and design disciplines, for example, Three-Dimensional Design and Graphic Design, and
2 Those that offer an art and design subject, such as fine art, together with a discipline from another academic field such as history or a language.

Included in this category would be degree courses that combine art history with another subject.

Over the last few years a number of new combined degree courses, embracing more than one field of art and design, have come into existence. These courses are normally listed, and considered separately, from the specialist courses grouped under the four main headings (Fine Art, Graphic Design, Textiles/Fashion, Three-Dimensional Design). Such courses allow for mobility between specialist subject areas and are helpful for students who cannot easily choose between different specialisms. While giving students the advantage of delaying a choice of specialisation, or of even maintaining two parallel subjects, there are disadvantages. If combined subjects are compatible and related, then attaining professional levels of competence may be possible. But if specialist talents are diffused across too many widely differing subjects, then attaining the level of professional expertise, necessary for employment in each subject, may be difficult.

If you are aiming towards employment in professional practice then it is necessary to choose groupings of practical subjects which are related and complementary. Alternatively, you may be seeking a broad mix of subjects, in which case professional vocational opportunities in industry may not be open to you. For example, graphic design and business studies may be ideal for design management, whereas silversmithing and interior design would appear hardly complementary and unlikely to equip you as a

College studies

working professional in either field.

Combined courses, in more than one art and design subject, therefore offer attractive and broad educational experiences, but need to be examined carefully if you are thinking in terms of a professional career in design. If you are equally interested, and able, in more than one subject, then choosing a combined degree can be very useful, but one must always balance such a decision with the problems of diluting study in one subject, to the detriment of subsequent specialist employment.

However, although much work in art and design is highly specialised, opportunities in related fields for people with a broader experience do exist. Such wider opportunities, in for example design management, arts administration, museums and galleries, art and design history, journalism, education and community arts are often ideally suited for people with multi-disciplinary qualifications. Alternatively, combined or multi-disciplinary courses may require further post-graduate study to provide an opportunity for specialist study following a broad based first degree.

While courses combining more than one practical art and design discipline are fairly rare—combined courses where art history or an art discipline (usually fine art) are studied along with another subject, are quite common. Such courses are normally found in the universities or the colleges of higher education and are not usually provided in the specialist colleges or faculties of art and design.

The history of art can be combined with a wide range of subjects, including languages, geography, drama, archaeology, music, philosophy and many other disciplines. The links with languages are particularly relevant especially if the language chosen relates to the area of art history being studied. Frequently a foreign language is a useful subsidiary subject because some historical texts are not available in English translation; some universities for this reason include a language as a compulsory subject.

Studies in fine art (and other art disciplines) are offered at a number of colleges and universities in association with an extremely broad range of subjects. For example, art and design can be combined with economics and mathematics, and fine art with languages, music, sociology, history and a diverse range of other disciplines. Combined courses of this nature normally lead to the award of an ordinary BA degree. Honours degrees are usually restricted to the specialist, single subject, art and design courses.

College studies

It is evident that the right choice of a subsidiary subject, or mix of subjects, is very important. The relationship between subjects is crucial if you are looking for a specific career outlet. Subsidiary or supporting subjects can enhance your career prospects if chosen carefully whereas a casual combination, while academically rich and exciting, may not necessarily relate to a specific job outlet. Choices on most combined courses are usually about the balance or relationship between the two, or at most three subjects. However, some recent modular courses offer an even wider choice with art and design forming a major component in large multi-disciplinary courses, covering a wide range of units or modules. There is clearly some debate concerning the role of combined and multi-disciplinary degrees. In the main they are seen as general degrees, without the specific career orientation of the specialist degrees. But a carefully considered, sensibly packaged mix, can have obvious benefits.

Full details of combined and multi-disciplinary courses are given in the Careers Research and Advisory Centre (CRAC) *Degree Course Guide: Art and Design including History of Art* and the CNAA *Directory of First Degree and Diploma of Higher Education Courses.*

(xi) The Diploma in higher education (DipHE)

This is a new type of course, with at present very few courses offering study opportunities in art and design. However, those that do exist provide a different style of study which may well suit particular needs.

The two year diploma is intended both as a terminal qualification in its own right and also as a course of study which, when successfully completed, provides the opportunity to proceed to further study, either leading to a degree or a professional qualification. All diplomas in higher education are at present awarded and validated by the CNAA and fall into a variety of patterns, being offered by different kinds of institutions.

The general principle underlying the creation of the DipHE was to provide an opportunity for students to study initially a wide range of subjects and have the chance to delay their subsequent choice of specialisation. This opportunity to delay their subject selection is to many the distinctive and attractive character of the DipHE. While the majority of DipHE courses provide a broad spectrum of choices a few remain specialist or vocational. The broader based diplomas are usually unit based or modular in structure, which means that a student may make up his or her own package of study from a number of different options, in several subjects. Such courses may offer a student a unique opportunity to

College studies

combine interests otherwise not available at degree level. Broader courses tend to place emphasis on developing a student's general competence rather than a distinct subject specialism.

The DipHE is recognised as the first two years of an honours degree, providing a student with the opportunity to either leave college with a diploma, in its own right, or to proceed or 'top up' the diploma with further study. The DipHE can be a helpful choice of course for those who cannot decide on a specific degree subject, or who want to combine art and design studies with other disciplines. However, it is important to make sure that there is provision for you to transfer to a degree course, or other appropriate exit route, once the DipHE is completed.

Grants for 'topping up' degree courses, after the DipHE, may not be given automatically if you need more than one year of further study. Transfer to the third and final year of a general degree course is usually possible, but you may need a further two years if you transfer onto a specialist course. You should check all transfer outlets for the DipHE very carefully when applying.

The normal requirement for entry to the DipHE is the same as for entry to a first degree course; although some courses are designed to particularly accommodate mature students. Many mature students find the DipHE a more flexible route into higher education since it initially involves a commitment of only two years. Any subsequent 'topping-up' of the DipHE can also normally occur at any future time—it does not necessarily have to follow immediately. This along with opportunities for part-time study often makes the DipHE attractive to more mature students.

Full details of the DipHE and the courses offered are contained in—The CNAA's *Directory of First Degree and Diploma of Higher Education Courses*.

5 Entry qualifications—how and when to apply

We have seen the wide variety of courses available in art and design and there is equally considerable variety in the entry requirements and methods of applying. Each type of course is therefore considered separately.

(i) Foundation course—entry requirements
When the foundation course is seen as the preliminary first year of an honours degree in art and design, then the academic qualifications, along with a folder of work, are the same for a degree (see (ii) below).

The foundation course may however lead onto a diploma course or further professional study so academic qualifications may

College studies

therefore vary. What does not vary is the need for a folder of work, providing evidence of your potential ability.

Normally, foundation course applicants should be at least 17 years of age on or before 1 October in the year of admission. Some courses, including two year foundation courses, will however accept students at an earlier age. Colleges offering early entry sometimes provide opportunity for study towards GCE subjects, to continue alongside work in art and design.

When and how to apply
Normally application is made in the autumn and spring terms, prior to the September when the course begins. It is important to apply early because popular courses may be full by January. Application in the first instance must be made to your nearest local college. Foundation courses may normally only be completed within your local authority area. Application forms should be obtained direct from your local college, to which forms are returned direct.

(ii) Specialist Art and Design Degrees (CNAA)
Entry requirements
For courses in professional, specialist studies, applicants must provide evidence of creative ability in art and design presented in a portfolio of work. In addition students are normally required to have completed a foundation course (or an approved DATEC diploma). The formal entry requirements for CNAA first degree courses in art and design are as follows:
(a) The satisfactory completion of a full-time foundation course in art and design of not less than one academic year, together with one of the following.
  (i) A GCE with passes in five subjects at 'O' level *or*
  (ii) A GCE with passes in four subjects including one at 'A' level.
(b) A GCE with passes in five subjects, including two subjects at 'A' level.
(c) A GCE with passes in four subjects, including three subjects at 'A' level.
(d) A Scottish Certificate of Education with passes in five subjects, of which three are at the Higher grade.
(e) A Scottish Certificate of Education with passes in four subjects, all at the Higher grade.
(f) An Ordinary National Certificate or Diploma at a good standard, or a DATEC Certificate or Diploma in Art and Design as specified by the relevant CNAA board or committee.

Passes at Grade 1 in the Certificate of Secondary Education are

College studies
considered as equivalent to Ordinary level GCE passes.

A Pass refers to grades A, B or C at Ordinary level.

Applicants in categories (b), (c), (d), (e) and (f) above may be considered for direct entry to a degree course, provided they have an outstanding folder of work, demonstrating evidence of practical creative ability. However, the normal and preferred route is through a foundation course. In exceptional cases applicants (normally mature students) of marked creative promise, capable of undertaking a degree course, may (at the discretion of the college) be admitted to a course without the minimum general educational requirements. Applicants should normally have reached the age of 18 before entry to a course.

Transfer onto the second or third years of degree courses, or admission to the first year may also be considered from students with a DATEC diploma or DipHE. DATEC general diplomas in many cases now include the work of former foundation courses and provide acceptable routes of entry to specialist degree courses.

How and when to apply
A central clearing house scheme—The Art and Design Admissions Registry, (ADAR) deals with all applications. All applications for forms are made in the January/February preceding the September in which the course starts, with a closing date of 31 March (when forms have to be at your first choice college). Students on foundation courses or at school cannot obtain individual forms direct from the registry. Principals of foundation course establishments and heads of secondary schools obtain forms for students from the registry.

Only applicants not in attendance at either an establishment of further education or a secondary school (external applicants) may obtain application forms direct from the registry. Requests for individual application forms should be made in January of the year of entry to the course—applications submitted after 31 March will only be considered in exceptional cases. Fuller details of the application procedures for specialist degree courses are contained in the CNAA's publication *First Degree Courses in Art and Design, Registration Scheme for Admission,* issued by The Association of Art Institutions, Art and Design Admissions Registry, Imperial Chambers, 24 Widemarsh Street, Hereford, HR4 9EP, details of entry requirements are also contained in the CNAA *Directory of First Degree and Diploma of Higher Education Courses,* available free of charge from the CNAA.

College studies

(iii) Non-specialist degrees at polytechnics and colleges of higher education
Courses in this category include degrees in the History of Art, combined courses, multi-disciplinary courses, and creative arts and cultural studies courses including elements of study in Art and Design.

Entry requirements
The normal minimum entry requirements for such courses is basically the same as those demanded by the universities. GCE qualifications with passes in five 'O' levels including two subjects at 'A' level (or the appropriate equivalent). Normally the requirement for a portfolio of work does not feature in the admission scheme for such non-specialist courses.

How and when to apply
Application forms are obtained from the college offering the course and returned directly to the institution. Forms are normally available, from colleges, from the autumn onwards. Colleges have their own closing dates but popular courses fill up quickly so early application is advisable. College prospectuses contain full details of entry requirements and admission procedures.

(iv) University degrees in art and design—including art history
Entry requirements
The basic minimum requirement is five GCE subjects including two at 'A' level (no subject to be counted at both levels). It cannot be too strongly stressed that these are only minimum requirements. What really counts is the quality of these results. Not all university departments use grades in quite the same way, some for instance fix a minimum grade below which no one is accepted. Further specific information must always therefore be obtained either from the particular university or from current publications. To be considered for admission to a university you must not only satisfy the 'general' requirement for the particular university concerned but also the 'course' requirement. Some History of Art courses require specific subjects such as a modern language or a qualification in art.

The folder of work is usually not so important when applying for most university courses, with their tendency towards more theoretical study. However, universities offering more practical and creative courses, while expecting the general academic requirement to be achieved, will also attach importance to a folio of practical work. There is a portfolio inspection scheme for most

College studies

fine art university degrees in which folders are sent to a London centre—details of this inspection scheme are obtainable from your first choice university.

How and when to apply

Applications to most universities should be made through the Universities Central Council on Admissions (UCCA). Forms are normally obtained from your school or direct from UCCA.

Applications to universities must be sent to UCCA by 15 December (Oxford or Cambridge by 15 October). Some universities consider that candidates who apply early (September/October) are more likely to be accepted. Application forms allow for up to six choices. Almost all universities are prepared to consider applicants who propose to spend an interim year before starting their course. They are also prepared usually to defer, for one year, any offer made to an applicant who decides, after being accepted, that they would wish to spend an interim year before starting a degree course.

Full details on application to university degree courses are contained in the UCCA handbook *How to Apply for Admission to a University*. This is published and revised annually in June and is essential to all applicants. It is available from The Universities Central Council on Admissions, PO Box 28, Cheltenham, Gloucester, GL50 1HY.

(v) DATEC—diplomas and certificates
Entry requirements

Entry requirements vary according to courses and subjects but your local college will be able to advise you on the subjects needed to enter a particular course. If you do not have the qualifications listed below, it may still be possible for you to be accepted on a DATEC course, at the discretion of the college, if you show a particular aptitude in your chosen area.

In addition to the academic qualifications set out it is also necessary to produce a folder of work, demonstrating your ability in art and design

DATEC Certificate—you should be aged sixteen or more and have at least three CSEs at grade III. The subjects required depend on the course chosen.

DATEC Diploma—you should be aged sixteen or more and normally have three 'O' level passes (grades A, B or C are usually required). However, you may be accepted with three CSEs at grade 1. The subjects required will depend on the course chosen.

College studies

DATEC Higher Certificate/Higher Diploma—you should be aged eighteen or more and possess a TEC art and design certificate or diploma. You may be able to enter a Higher Certificate or Higher Diploma course if you have suitable GCE 'O' levels and/or 'A' levels, in which case additional studies may be necessary. Entry may also be direct from a satisfactorily completed foundation course.

How and when to apply
Application forms and details of entry requirements, and admission procedures, are available from your local college—and always appear in the college prospectus.

Applications are normally considered in the spring and summer terms prior to the course commencing in September, but as with all courses early contact with your local college is advisable.

As from 1982 the Art and Design Admissions Registry (ADAR—the Clearing House for the BA (Hons) Art and Design degree courses) will operate a national scheme for recruitment onto DATEC Higher Diploma courses.

(vi) Art teacher training
Entry requirements
Minimum entry requirements to BEd courses in education (with art and design as options) are five GCE passes, two of which must be at 'A' level. As from 1984 all entrants to teaching posts will need to have GCE 'O' levels in English and Mathematics, or otherwise show proof of competence in these subjects.

If considering options in Craft, Design and Technology it is desirable that one of the 'A' levels is in CDT or a related design subject.

Candidates who already possess suitable industrial experience and hold a national diploma or OND, HNC or Higher Technician award may be eligible for entry to BEd courses including a shortened two year course.

Holders of the DipHE may also qualify for a shortened one or two year BEd course. If considering specialising in Art and Craft, on a BEd course, GCE passes in art and design would be helpful and you may be required, in some instances, to show examples of your work.

Entry to post-graduate certificate courses in Education (PGCE) and Art Teachers Certificates or Diplomas (ATC/D) are open to students holding the appropriate first degrees.

How and when to apply
BEd degree courses, of initial teacher training, are offered in

College studies

university departments of education and in polytechnics and colleges of higher education.

For the courses offered in university departments applications should be made through the Universities Central Council of Admissions (UCCA) not later than 15 December (15 October for Oxford or Cambridge).

The Central Register and Clearing House Limited handles all applications for courses of intitial teacher training outside the universities. The first step in applying for a place on a teacher training course is to write to the college of your choice—who will then send you the necessary enquiry card (MW Card). Students then submit this card to the Central Register and Clearing House Ltd, 3 Crawford Place, London, W1H 2BN, in order to receive application forms and an information booklet.

You should complete the forms the Clearing House provides and send them to the institution of your choice, with the necessary registration fee. This fee covers the cost of passing on the application form to other colleges, if you are not accepted by the college of your first choice.

Forms are available from 15 September, a year ahead of entry. There is no official closing date for the registration scheme but it obviously helps to apply early. Students applying for entry to teacher training courses in Scotland should apply direct to the college concerned.

Application forms for post-graduate teacher training (PGCE and ATC/D) are available from your college, if still in attendance, if not PGCE application forms are available from the Graduate Teacher Training Registry, 3 Crawford Place, London, W1H 2BN, or for ATC/D courses from the Clearing House for post-graduate courses in Art Education, The Manor House, Heather, Leicesterhsire, LE6 1QP. Application forms from October onwards.

(vii) College diplomas and certificates, post-graduate courses in Art and Design, Engineering courses

Entry requirements and procedures for admission for courses in this category generally come within the schemes already outlined but some brief further reference may be helpful.

Requirements for college validated courses vary and information can only be obtained from individual college prospectuses. Regional Advisory Councils (See Addresses on page 149) however publish lists of courses, with basic entry requirements, but early contact with specific colleges is advisable.

Engineering courses related to study towards engineering design come under several categories. University degree courses in

College studies

engineering come under the UCCA scheme already discussed, while details of all CNAA engineering degree courses are obtainable from polytechnics and colleges. Some industrial design (Engineering) courses also come within the ADAR scheme for specialist Art and Design degree courses, covered in section (ii) above.

In addition to degrees, a wide range of Higher and Ordinary Diplomas and Certificates in engineering are awarded by the Technician Education Council—details of which can be obtained from local colleges or the Technician Education Council, 76 Portland Place, London, W1N 4AA.

There are in addition to studies at first degree level, numerous post-graduate courses in art and design. These range from taught courses, to individual research programmes.

Details of entry to such courses are held by colleges offering first degrees and students normally obtain full information while studying for their first degree. Entry to post-graduate courses is dependent on having obtained a first degree, normally at an appropriate level, and the ability to demonstrate that your talent and ability would justify further study and research. Entry to many post-graduate courses, particularly at centres such as the Royal College of Art and the Slade School, is extremely competitive.

Full details of Masters Courses in Design subjects are found in the Design Council's booklet *Design Courses in Great Britian* CNAA post-graduate courses are listed in the Council's booklet.

6 Grants

Grants, or local education authority awards, given to students for full-time study, depend on many things including changes in the economic climate, and the present situation is very uncertain due to cuts in local authority budgets.

It is essential that you find out, as early as possible, whether you are eligible for a grant. You should make a grant application to your local education authority (LEA) as soon as you decide to enter higher education. Do not wait for a firm place at a college before applying for an award. Application forms, and further details about local authority awards, are available from the Chief Education Officer at the local authority for the area in which you live.

There are two types of grant; mandatory and discretionary awards. A mandatory award means that the LEA is obliged to give you a major award; while a discretionary award means that the LEA is not obliged to give you an award and if they do, the amount varies according to the LEA's discretion. A mandatory grant is normally awarded for a period of three years.

College studies

You are eligible for a mandatory award if (*a*) you are taking a full-time or sandwich degree course, a TEC or BEC Higher Diploma, a Higher National Diploma (HND), a Diploma in Higher Education (DipHE) or a course of initial teacher training (all post 'A' level courses); (*b*) you have been ordinarily resident in the British Isles for three years prior to beginning the course; (*c*) you have not previously undertaken one or more courses of full-time higher education for more than one term's duration.

Students who do not meet these requirements, or who are on courses that are not included in (a) above, may be able to obtain an award at the discretion of their local authority. From the list of courses meriting mandatory awards it will be seen that all diplomas or certificate courses which can be entered below the age of 18 are excluded. Such 'lower level' courses usually only merit discretionary awards, as does the foundation course and most local authorities will now not consider financing you to study on a foundation course outside their area. Courses with mandatory awards may be studied within any authority and you are therefore not restricted to your local area for advanced level work.

Awards paid by local authorities to students attending courses of higher education cover examination and tuition fees, plus a sum for materials and maintenance; somewhere to live, food, books and travel. A mandatory major award covers all these elements of expense, while a discretionary award is likely to cover, for instance, only tuition and other examination fees, with perhaps a contribution towards travel or other expenses. It will therefore be apparent that discretionary awards are for example usually made for home based study, for students under 18 or for lower level courses within your local authority. If you are only eligible for a discretionary award then it is particularly important to apply early. Some local authorities have closing dates for discretionary awards several months before courses begin, after which they will not consider further awards. This is usually on 31 May but can be as early as the end of March, particularly if resources are short.

All students' grants are assessed according to parental income. Depending on income, parents have to make a contribution on your award, or to put it another way, the local authority deducts from your award what it calculates your parents could afford to contribute. Grants are not assessed according to parental income if the student has independent status and is single, in which case no parental contribution is required and maximum grant is paid. A student is classified as being independent if he or she has supported themselves for three years prior to the commencement of the course or are 25 years of age or older. If you are 25 during your course you acquire independent status from the beginning of

College studies

the academic year following your 25th birthday. A student also has independent status if he or she is married in which case the husband or wife's income is used to assess the amount of grant on the same basis as parental income. The fees portion of your award is sent direct to your college while the maintenance portion is sent by cheque to you and incidentally you have to apply for each year's grant on your course separately.

The following list sets out the general eligibility of courses for grants:

Foundation course—Discretionary awards only with most local authorities not financing study outside their area.

College validated vocational certificates and diplomas, DATEC Diplomas, Certificates and Higher Certificates—Discretionary awards; with many LEAs not financing study outside their area unless the course or subject you wish to study is not offered at a local institution. Your local authority or college should be able to tell you what type of award the course you have applied for merits.

Degrees (full-time and sandwich) DATEC Higher Diplomas, DipHE, Courses of initial teacher training—Mandatory grants with students normally eligible for major awards. Students on a sandwich course who spend part of an academic year in industry receive a grant for the period they spend in College only. Normally the period in industry is covered by a 'wage' from the 'employee', broadly equivalent in level to the students grant.

Post-graduate teacher training courses (ATC/D/PGCE)
This is normally considered as a period of initial teacher training with students eligible for an award from their local authority.

Post-graduate study—higher degrees
Normally only discretionary awards are made by LEAs. For some courses you may qualify for a post-graduate bursary or studentship from the Department of Education and Science (DES). Application for such bursaries is made through the college offering the post-graduate course at the time you apply for the course. Some courses are recognised for a certain number of DES bursaries and without this support students need to be self-financing or in receipt of a scholarship or industrial bursarship, or sponsored by industry for specific research. Much post-graduate work, including both taught courses and individual research, is offered on a part-time basis. If registered as a part-time students, over a large period, you will generally be able to support yourself with part-time work while continuing your study.

Full information concerning grants should be available from your school careers office or local library. Two booklets: *Getting*

Working as a designer, craftsman or artist
a *Grant* and *Grants to Students* are available from the Department of Education and Science, Information Division, Elizabeth House, York Road, London, SE1 7PH, or from your local careers teacher or local education authority.

4 Working as a designer, craftsman or artist

1 Introduction

There is a world of difference between working as an art student and working as an artist or designer; even in an area, such as art and design, where study takes the form of practical work related to industrial needs.

Art college life is fundamentally supportive. Staff are available to offer help and advice, like-minded fellow students surround you; you get help with the supply of materials and, more important than anything, you have space to work in—which is heated and lit for you—with no rent to pay. Moving from these sympathetic surroundings to the frequent isolation of work is not always easy. Post-graduate studies and further advanced research, supported by bursaries, may help as an initial buffer, and further prepare you for work, but sooner or later we are faced with the problem of establishing ourselves as a working artist, designer or craftsman.

One characteristic of working in art and design is the independent nature of so much of the work. You as an individual have to establish a market for your work and ideas—only in certain areas do you slot into a supportive, already established industrial structure. More often than not you are seeking to work on your own and establish yourself as an independent artist or designer.

Success in a talent industry depends on how good you are. In general, no national framework exists, with clearly advertised posts, and career opportunities, ready for all designers to step into. You have to either find an outlet for your talent or even create a new market for your ideas, and what it is you have to sell. It is one thing to work for years in the partially cloistered walls of an art school, and quite another virtually to have to invent and establish your own existence.

There are obviously areas of the art and design industry where a professional job structure exists, into which designers fit. But

Working as a designer, craftsman or artist

outlets for a great majority of creative work have to be discovered, invented and established by the craftsman-designer himself.

Inventing your own existence, as it were, calls for a great deal of determination and tenacity. Whether it is realistic, in the present economic climate, to expect to make a living in your chosen profession certainly depends on the determination of the individual, as much as on his or her training. Not only is art and design a 'talent' industry in which competition for work is very much controlled by the quality of what you have to offer—it is also a 'fashion' industry susceptible to changes in public fashion and private taste. The demand for your work may therefore not be constant. What may attract commissions when you first leave college, because your ideas are fresh and fashionable, may not be what is wanted in a few years time. Work in art and design does not generally follow a smooth and constant development; like promotion and progression in other industries. Artists and designers must continue, at all times to develop new ideas and be willing to change their ideas, and adapt or respond to what may be required by the changing demands of industry or the public.

Although your ideas and work may be fresh and attractive, getting started as a working designer can be very difficult. The most common problem is the need to have in your portfolio examples of work which has actually been produced or manufactured commercially. Prospective clients clearly want to see what you are capable of and whether other people have had sufficient confidence in you to produce or buy your designs. Getting started is therefore difficult and often frustrating. Work for designers so often goes to those already with experience or with evidence in their portfolios of completed commissions. More will be said later in this section on approaches to getting started, as it varies according to which field you may wish to work in, but evidence of something actually printed or produced, however modest, is more important than all the brilliant ideas you may have in your folder. This probably suggests that to begin with you must not be too 'choosey'. Rather than turn down a job, because it does not offer much creative scope, you should jump at any offer to get your work produced; in this way you can demonstrate to prospective employers and clients that not only do you have ideas but you are capable of seeing a job through to the end and producing the required goods, however mundane and humble, at the time required.

That is what employers want—the job delivered on time to their specification. Scope for your own creativity can occur later when you have secured a job, or established a market for your ideas. Too often, when young designers start work, they only want to be

Working as a designer, craftsman or artist

concerned with work that gives full range to their new and bright creative ideas and turn down offers for routine work.

The amount of so-called creativity in any job varies and often it is only a very small proportion. What matters most of all is responding positively to the demands and requirements of the client and user and getting what is required produced within a tight financial budget and deadline.

In reality jobs are given to artists and designers on the evidence of the work in their portfolios not on the level of their academic qualifications (though good level passes obviously help in a competitive world).

The evidence employers are looking for is not only bright ideas and talent—that is only part of it—but evidence of your ability to produce the goods when the manufacturer or client needs them.

Once your folder contains some examples of produced and manufactured work to support your creative ideas, then employment opportunities will gradually expand. It is therefore essential that as part of getting started you accept any opportunity to get your work produced, however mundane such early jobs may appear after all the apparently exciting ideas you have worked on in college.

College leavers not only have to compete with experienced designers, with commercially produced work already safely in their portfolios, but also may sometimes have to compete with experienced people who have been taken on straight from school and trained within the industry rather than at college. The college leaver may have the creative ideas and the theory but, in harsh economic reality, he must be prepared to take on routine work and start learning some things from the bottom up. The graduate or college diplomate has to realise that his training, however orientated to industry, still leaves him with a great deal to learn about basic industrial and day to day commercial and production practice.

The United Kingdom trains more artists and designers than any other European country. There are therefore a great number of young designers looking for jobs each year. Some people may say that too many designers and craftsmen are trained, while others will argue that if we are going to succeed as a manufacturing country, and if the quality of our lives and surroundings are to be improved, then we cannot have enough creative and practical people on the job market.

Whatever the truth (and the Department of Education and Science keeps a close watch on student numbers) there are, each year, a great number of young college leavers looking for only a few openings.

It is therefore all highly competitive and success will depend on how good you are and how prepared you are to start at a basic production level, after all the high hopes of a graduation exhibition.

The last official Government survey on the employment of art college leavers was published in 1970—based on statistics collected in 1968. This survey reported that some 70% of design students (not including fine art) found jobs in appropriate design work with a very high proportion (81%) in graphic design.

The economic situation has changed since then and the current depression has not helped designers—who traditionally tend to be treated as unnecessary luxuries when times are hard. However, at a time of widespread unemployment it is probably true to say that opportunities for design students are no worse than for other graduates—in fact probably better (as they were in 1968) particularly when one bears in mind that a creative training (such as art and design) equips young people to be imaginative, tenacious and inventive. Such qualities frequently help art students to recognise and exploit the potential range of activities which require the skills of the creative and practical person.

Many young people when getting started will of course take on other supporting employment. Part-time teaching used to offer such support but, as we have seen, much of this has been eroded by cuts in public expenditure. However, many other forms of casual or part-time work are often used by young craftsmen and designers to help them through the early days of establishing themselves and finding a market for their skills and ideas.

2 Where will you work? Two broad categories

(i) Freelance designer or (ii) Staff designer

The nature of work in art and design is diverse and conditions vary enormously from field to field. Generally, however, you will either work on your own at home, as a freelance designer/artist, or alternatively 'go to work' in a design studio or office. In other words you will either be a 'staff designer' working office like hours in a studio or drawing office or work independently at home for a variety of clients, who may commission work from you.

Most designed products we see around us are mainly the result of designers working on a freelance basis. In other words the great majority of firms and industries do not necessarily employ a full-time designer, or design team, but commission freelance work from a designer when any of their products need redesigning or improving, or when they need to consider a new product. Manufacturers may then 'consult' a specialist designer or team of designers—hence the phrase 'consultant' designer—meaning someone industry brings in to consult with.

The employment of designers, as we shall see, depends on the type of industry. Some industries such as publishing and printing constantly require designers and therefore usually have permanent design offices staffed by professional designers. Other industries may only need designers at infrequent intervals, in their production cycle, and therefore employ freelance or consultant designers as and when they are needed. A crude guideline to the varying demand industries make on designers may be illustrated by considering the permanence of products. In simple terms industries such as printing, advertising or exhibition design, whose products have a short life, obviously require designers more regularly to redesign new things. For example, we throw away much printed material—it is ephemeral and impermanent, and the demand for new material is constant. Think of television advertisements, not only do we constantly need new images and ideas but the product only lasts a few seconds on our screens.

Other products, however, like refrigerators and furniture last much longer and are less frequently redesigned. We do not throw settees away like bus tickets, so industries dealing with more permanent commodities tend to use freelance designers, on an occasional basis, rather than employ a large full-time design staff. Exceptions of course are in the field of technological design such as the aircraft and motor industries and electronics where the demands of technology may require permanent design research teams working on long term design policies.

The designer's work therefore varies from industry to industry and in terms of whether he is working as a freelance designer or a permanent staff designer. Similarly, the problems facing the artist and craftsman are different from those of the designer.

The pattern of employment depends not only on your professional specialisation but on whether you are trained as an artist, designer or craftsman. There is, as we have seen, a wide variety of activities ranging from the fine artist to the industrial product designer and we need therefore to examine the two broadly differing categories of 'designer' and 'artist-craftsman', a little more fully.

There is obviously considerable overlap between the roles of artists, craftsman and designer but it is self-evident that in broad terms designers are for example more likely to work in design offices and studios; while craftsmen and artists more usually work on their own at home or in their own workshop. It is however worth exploring, in a little more detail some of the fundamental differences.

Working as a designer, craftsman or artist

3 The industrial designer

In this context let us think of the industrial designer as a person who designs for industry—any industry, from textiles to advertising and from furniture to publishing or fashion. The industrial designer does not make the product; he works with other people in a production team contributing his skills in terms of the shape and appearance of the product, and an understanding of the users' requirements. Generally to do this work the designer must leave his home and join others in a design office. He may be employed full-time by one industry or company, or he may have his own office and act as a freelance consultant to a number of companies.

Full-time jobs in design offices are advertised and can be found in professional journals and some daily newspapers (see details on page 142). However, the number of jobs advertised does not reflect the amount of work for designers, in fact advertisements for posts in some industries are quite rare. And when advertisements do occur all too frequently they ask for candidates 'with experience'. This dilemma has already been referred to and the need to get some evidence of production experience in your portfolio is the vital first step. Two ways of gaining experience are either to take on modest freelance work, or start in industry at a lower position than an honours graduate may sometimes expect to begin.

Freelance work can be seen in two ways: those initial contracts you may receive early in your career which give you the opportunity, however modest, to demonstrate your ability in production terms. This may then lead to a full-time appointment—as the freelance work gives you the experience the advertisements so often require.

The other type of freelance work is that which one takes on as an established and experienced designer. As already mentioned, a great deal of design work is the result of freelance commissions and consultant designers, working either individually or in groups, are able to build up a practice which can demand high professional fees from a range of clients. Such freelance practice is clearly the ambition of many designers but frequently designers need experience in a design office, as a staff designer, building up a reputation, before they are able to set up in private practice.

A pattern, or cycle, of employment therefore emerges. This may begin with a few modest freelance commissions, which can lead to full-time design office work. This in turn can give you the necessary experience to subsequently set up in more well paid freelance practice.

Working as a designer, craftsman or artist

Entering a design office direct from college may be difficult, without the experience already referred to, but those opportunities which do exist often require the young designer to start at the bottom and carry out routine work. So many designers have had to start their careers, after leaving college, as a junior in a lowly position—but it is this experience, making one more realistic, which is essential and part of becoming a designer.

College leavers need to realise that their degree or diploma does not necessarily qualify them for immediate entry into the world of design. There is still much to be done in terms of establishing yourself. You may, as we have seen, have to initially take on routine work, and as a freelance designer you will need to take your portfolio round to prospective employers—touting for custom. After you have done some work as a freelance designer you will probably begin to build up a list of regular clients—providing your work has been satisfactory. After that you will possibly not need to sell yourself so much—word will travel that you are reliable and do good work. Though of course once you have started you still have to maintain the flow of creative work and ideas—clients only choose you because you do good work and meet deadlines, however well established you may become.

Careers obviously do not follow a stereotype common pattern and your work may go in all manner of directions once you have got started. What is important however is getting started and we have looked at two possibilities—modest freelance work to gain experience, or accepting a full-time post with the likelihood of the work initially being rather routine or lowly.

Early freelance work may be slow to turn up and young designers may invariably need to do other work to support themselves while waiting for the first commissions. This supporting work normally has to be part-time, as you need to have time to pursue all possibilities, taking your portfolio around as many clients as possible, and continuing work on your own ideas at the same time.

This period, immediately after leaving college, can be depressing and you are likely to need all the determination, commitment and confidence in your own talent that took you to art school in the first place.

Many young college leavers find support during this difficult interim period by setting up with a group of other young designers. Much industrial design work is in fact undertaken by *group practices*. A group practice is one where designers, usually in similar fields of work, set up as freelance consultants. The advantages of shared resources and expenses are self evident but a

Working as a designer, craftsman or artist

further advantage is that a variety of skills and disciplines in a group can have more chance of attracting work than one young designer working in isolation. Designing is normally a group activity anyhow, calling for a variety of different skills. If these are combined in a group the likelihood of attracting commissions may therefore be enhanced.

Established and renowned designers set up group practices and normally these are seen as the top end of the profession. In recent years however young designers have realised that this method of operating, and of attracting freelance work, is very helpful when beginning a career. Not only may a group be more economically viable, and have collectively more to offer, but the association of like-minded ex-students helps bridge the gap from student life to design practice.

Setting up such practices requires, not only some money, but legal and financial advice. Some knowledge of basic business practice is therefore essential and many design courses now include such studies. Professional bodies, including, for example the Society of Industrial Artists and Designers, and commercial organisations such as Artlaw, also offer advice and answer queries. Details of organisations which can help are set out on page 151.

Freelance designers, in addition to taking their portfolios to prospective clients and companies, can also publicise themselves through advertising in selected journals and professional handbooks. Further publicity may be obtained through acceptance and inclusion in the Design Council or Society of Industrial Artists and Designers' (SIAD) designer registers.

(i) Employing an agent

Getting started as a freelance designer is difficult and subsequently finding further work (before you are well enough known for people to come to you) takes up a lot of time.

In order to sell drawings and designs, and obtain commissions, many designers use the services of an artist's agent. Agents do not operate in every field but are common in the world of graphics, fashion design and textiles. The agent's job is to find work for his clients and he has contacts with industry and potential customers, to whom examples of your work will be shown.

An agent will of course only take on designers and artists who he considers have the ability to produce and maintain high quality work which he can sell. If accepted by an agent then it is his job to find work, he will also arrange the payment of fees, and can often get more than the young artist, who may not necessarily be a good business person. The agent also usually deals with invoices and statements and the problem of the customer who is slow to settle

Working as a designer, craftsman or artist

his account. For all this the agent of course charges a fee, normally ranging from 10-25% of all payments made to the artist.

If the young freelance designer chooses not to use an agent, or cannot find an agent interested in his work, then the designer has to study the potential market carefully and find out which organisations may use his type of work. The designer must then visit art directors, buyers, design managers or staff designers and show them his portfolio. Most of these people will usually find time to see a designer's work, they are after all, always looking for new talent and ideas. Such interviews are very important because, even if one company or firm cannot use your work, they are likely to either give you valuable professional advice or suggest other possible buyers.

4 Artists and designer-craftsmen

Artists and craftsmen work differently from designers. The primary difference is that the artist or craftsman is responsible for the total production process—he designs and makes (as well as all the other tasks) whereas the designer designing for industrial production is only responsible for part of the process. In addition designers usually work as part of a team while an artist or craftsman normally works alone. Employment patterns and the problems of getting started after leaving college, are therefore different for artists and craftsmen.

(i) Outlets for work
Unlike the designer the craftsperson or fine artist has to find his own commercial outlets for his products. The designer, once he is commissioned by industry, has to submit his designs but does not have to worry about the marketing and distribution of the final manufactured product. The craftsperson and artist does—having made something, whether it is a pot, piece of jewellery or a painting he must then find an outlet or market for it.

In recent years there has been a craft boom, encouraged by, among other things, the growth of tourism and a certain disenchantment in the consumer market with sterotyped mass produced goods. This boom has increased the range and number of commercial outlets for the crafts and certainly in major cities, and particularly in London and the South East, retail outlets for hand made craftwork are widespread.

The variety of outlets range from galleries and shops to market stalls and exhibitions. The energetic craftsperson needs to explore a variety of places where work may be sold—art and craft shops, large stores, craft markets and even banks, colleges and places of

Working as a designer, craftsman or artist

business which will, from time to time, show examples of craft work for sale.

Having found a retail outlet whether it is a large store or a market stall, you have then to guarantee that you are able to produce further work in response to sales. In other words you need a place to work. It is no good leaving some of your college produced work at a shop and then not being able to meet, or follow up, any orders for further work. People selling your work must know whether you are in a position to produce further copies and respond to orders with more work. You must therefore be in a position where you can continue working and build up stock.

(ii) A place to work
So the first problem is to find a place to work. This depends on the craft you practice. Some work can easily be carried out at your home, and space can be adapted so that production may be undertaken. This is fine with crafts such as embroidery or knitting and jewellery but other work such as sculpture, furniture or ceramics requires larger specialist workshop space. Working at home though can be ideal if you have the basic materials and facilities.

College leavers frequently not only feel isolated but miss the facilities and access to machinery they enjoyed at college. You may therefore need not only to purchase equipment, basic machinery and tools but also find somewhere to work. If you need access to expensive equipment such as printing presses, kilns or photographic resources then joining an existing workshop or studio may help.

Regional Arts Associations can usually give you information and put you in touch with artists and craftsmen working in groups or already sharing facilities. A large number of craft workshops have recently been opened, frequently in old warehouses or large disused buildings, where groups of artists have developed collective schemes to rent accommodation, sharing the basic costs and providing access to equipment and machinery.

A base of this nature not only offers a place to work but also provides a site where your work can be exhibited and viewed by prospective customers. If you are working at home you tend to have to take your work around to all possible buyers whereas if you have a studio, or share a workshop, the public and potential clients can come and see your work in suitable surroundings.

If you cannot rent space in a collective craft studio or workshop you may at least find that facilities and machinery may be used at a reasonable charge.

Some grants are available to help craftsmen obtain studios and a

Working as a designer, craftsman or artist

number of organisations, set out on page 151 exist to help young designer-craftsmen find suitable accommodation.

Local authorities are sometimes helpful, particularly if groups of craftsmen have schemes for using short life property, due for eventual demolition, or can fit into any local urban renewal schemes by using disused stores or warehouses.

(iii) Craftsmen and freelance industrial designers

As we have pointed out earlier, craftsmen normally work as designer-craftsmen—that is, designing objects as well as actually producing them. Craftsmen however may also design for industry and combine the activities of 'craftsmen-designer' with 'industrial designer'. A craftsmen can therefore in addition to producing hand made objects, for direct retail outlets, also act as a freelance designer for industry—if he or she has the necessary skills; in this way the range of potential work can of course be extended.

The breadth of attitude to work in art and design, where narrow barriers between hand skills and industrial production are broken down, obviously enhances employment opportunities for young craftsmen and designers.

(iv) Exhibiting

In addition to finding retail outlets in shops and other places there are a large number of galleries, throughout the country, where opportunities to exhibit work may be found.

It is essential for the young artist or craftsmen to get his work in front of the public as much as possible—exposure to the buying public is one way of getting known and started. The large fashionable galleries are obviously difficult to interest but there are many smaller and provincial galleries, dealing in art and craft, which offer space to young artists. Open exhibitions and competitions are always advertised in the art press and young artists should take every chance to enter work.

(v) Grants

Grants to help artists and craftsmen set up workshops and get their careers started are available, though not particularly plentiful. Rather like the prospective industrial designer needing to demonstrate that he has experience, before he is given a job, the craftsman or artist will also have to demonstrate that he has proven ability, and has continued work since leaving college.

Awarding agencies will usually require evidence demonstrating your development as an artist or craftsman, and will possibly expect you to have shown or exhibited your work publicly. We can all produce work when supported by a college but what matters,

Working as a designer, craftsman or artist

particularly to anyone likely to sponsor you or buy your work, is proof that you can continue working on your own.

Regional Arts Associations, the Arts Council and Crafts Council all have schemes for providing assistance and finance for the creative arts and crafts and further details and addresses are given on page 150. The Arts Council publishes a guide to Awards and Schemes. These include a limited number of studio grants and a bursary scheme for the purchase or commission of works of art.

The Arts Council supports a wide range of creative arts, including painting, sculpture, photography, printmaking and film.

The Crafts Council supports and promotes the work of artists-craftsmen, in all manner of crafts, and award a limited number of Workshop Training grants to help established craftsmen take on young craftsmen for workshop experience. The Council also awards grants, loans or bursaries to new craftsmen.

Young craftsmen and artists should always ensure that they read the specialist art and craft press and national journals. In these publications information is carried on the whole range of trusts, bursaries and competitions set up to help artists. Independent charities, colleges, industrial companies and foundations often support the arts by making awards, or offering scholarships, bursaries, fellowships or sponsored exhibitions to young artists.

5 Legal and financial advice – setting up a business on your own

Both the industrial designer and craftsman are likely to find themselves working on their own, setting up either individual or group practices. The craft industry is particularly suited to small business units and the growth in recent years of small industries has contributed substantially to the national economy.

Rather ironically today's high unemployment, job insecurity and abundance of mass-produced artefacts have all encouraged people to have the confidence to, as it were, 'go it alone'. Redundancy payments have given many people, who may have previously practised a craft as a hobby, the impetus to start their own venture and second career. But more significantly, as so many normal employment patterns no longer offer long term security, the ideal of starting your own business may often now appear a more attractive option.

Setting up your own workshop and business does however bring with it financial and legal problems including for example contracts with galleries and suppliers, income tax and VAT returns, copyright, tenancy agreements and many other things which may seem a long way away from a creative career training.

Hopefully you may have been given some help in these

Some specific occupations—a broad guide

important formal matters while at college. But there are a number of organisations and professional bodies giving advice to artists and craftsmen. Advice must be obtained as no small business can survive without this support.

Some addresses and details of organisations are given on page 151 and a book list on page 145.

5 Some specific occupations – A broad guide

As we have seen jobs in art and design do not always fit neatly into self-contained compartments. Jobs and skills frequently overlap, and the boundaries of each occupation cannot always be clearly defined. One of the reasons for this is the broad, all embracing nature of design—affecting so many aspects of our lives, and the very large number of manufactured products and goods which we use, and which all have to be designed. Any clear classification of jobs is therefore not easy and is, in some cases, a little artificial. However this section sets out to provide a broad guide to jobs—what people do, and what all the different titles for occupations actually mean.

The occupations are listed under the traditional four broad categories of Graphic Design, Three-Dimensional Design, Textiles/Fashion and Fine Art, with a brief section on Art Teaching. The specific occupations considered in this section are mainly those which can be defined and, in general, advertised as full-time posts. The whole range of freelance work, not easily classified, and as diverse as any designer's ideas, or clients commission, is not included.

1 Graphic Design

Graphic Design, concerned with communicating information and ideas by a combination of words and images, is certainly the largest area of design training and many specialised occupations are related to it. The activities and work of the graphic designer are wide and varied—work frequently overlaps from one field to another and most occupations require at least a working knowledge, or experience, in a variety of graphic specialisms. Graphic design, as we have seen, is mainly associated with the advertising, publishing, printing and communication industries, and a basic knowledge of printing technology and image production systems is essential. Many jobs require an all round

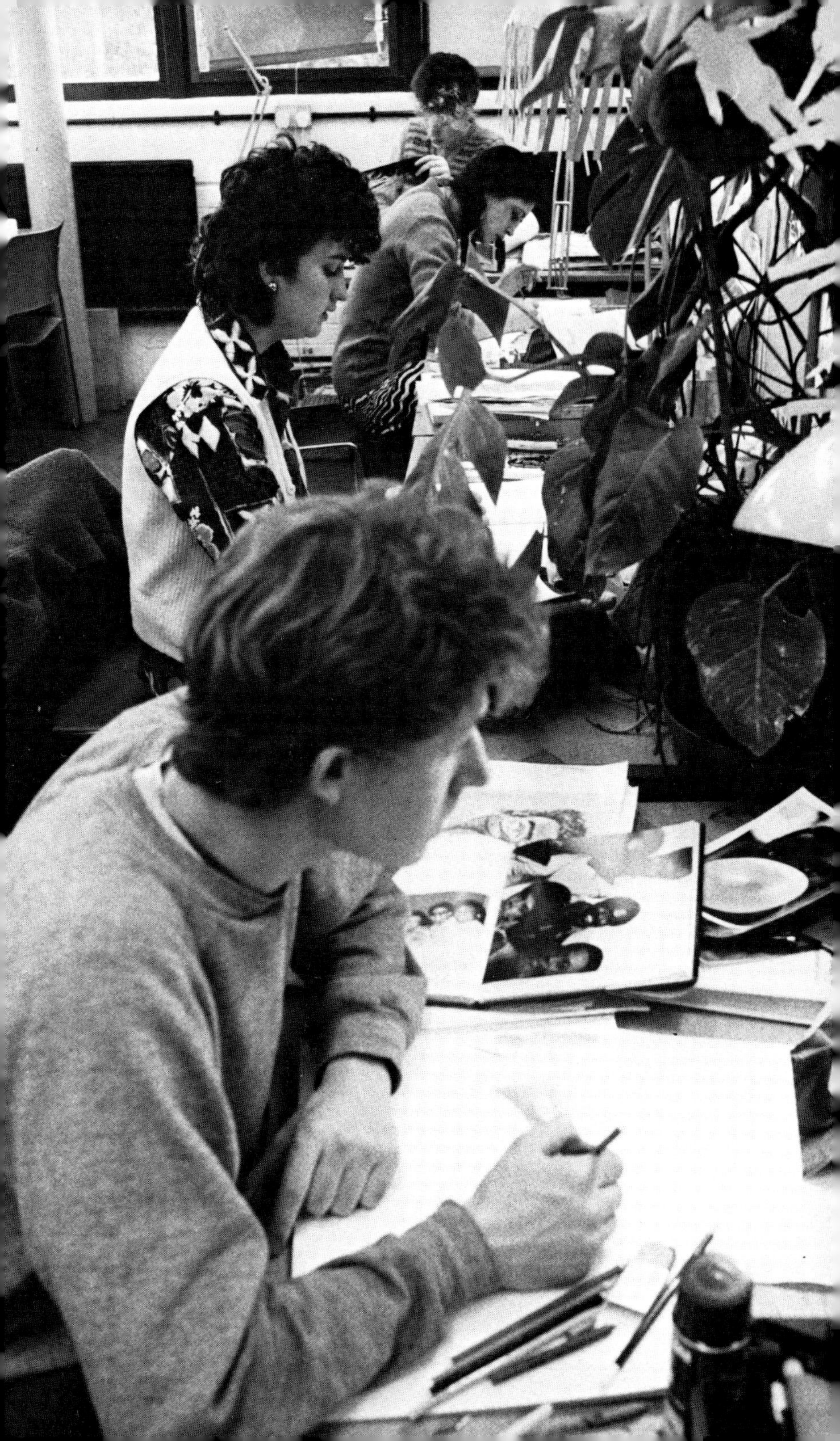

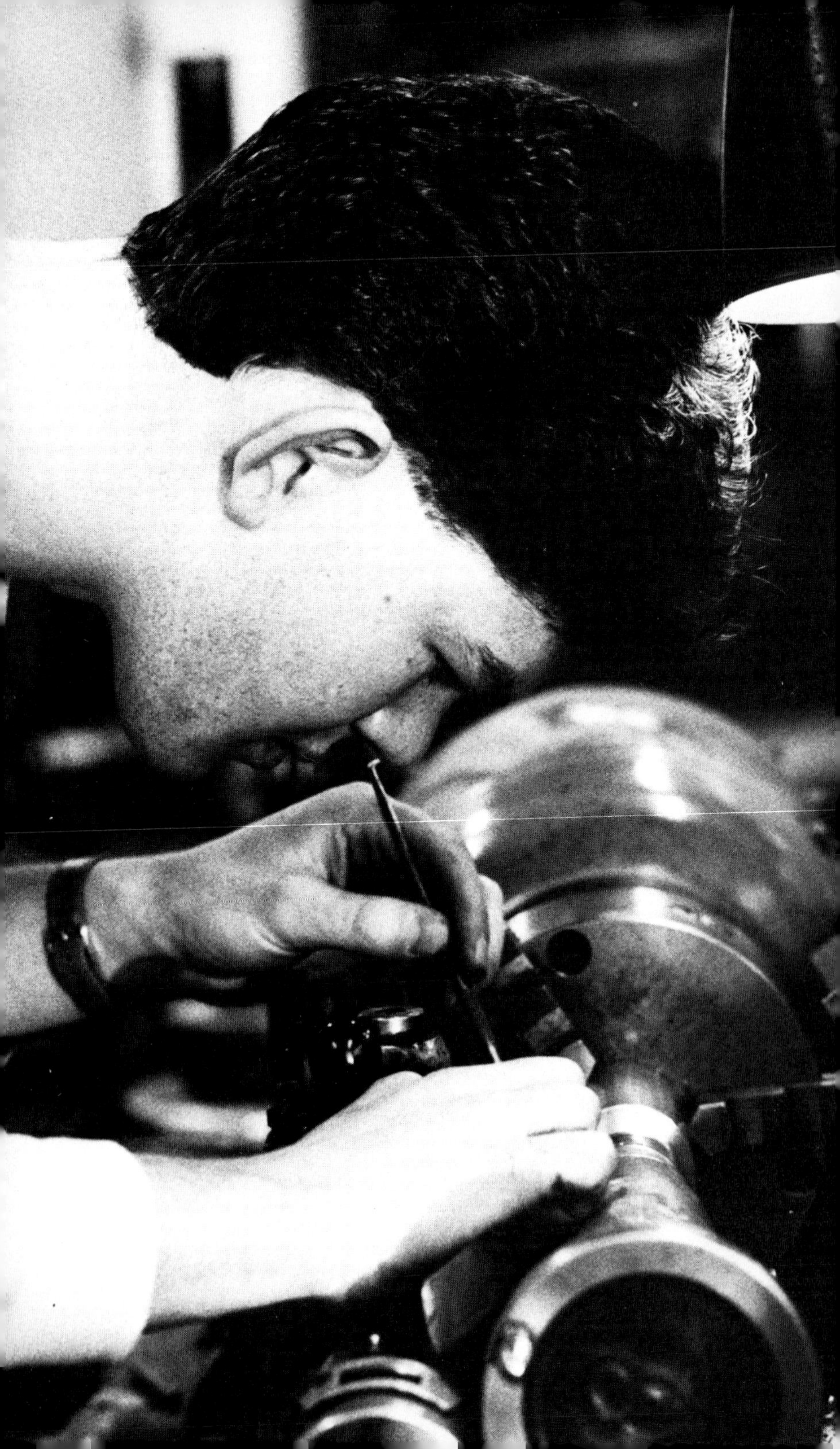

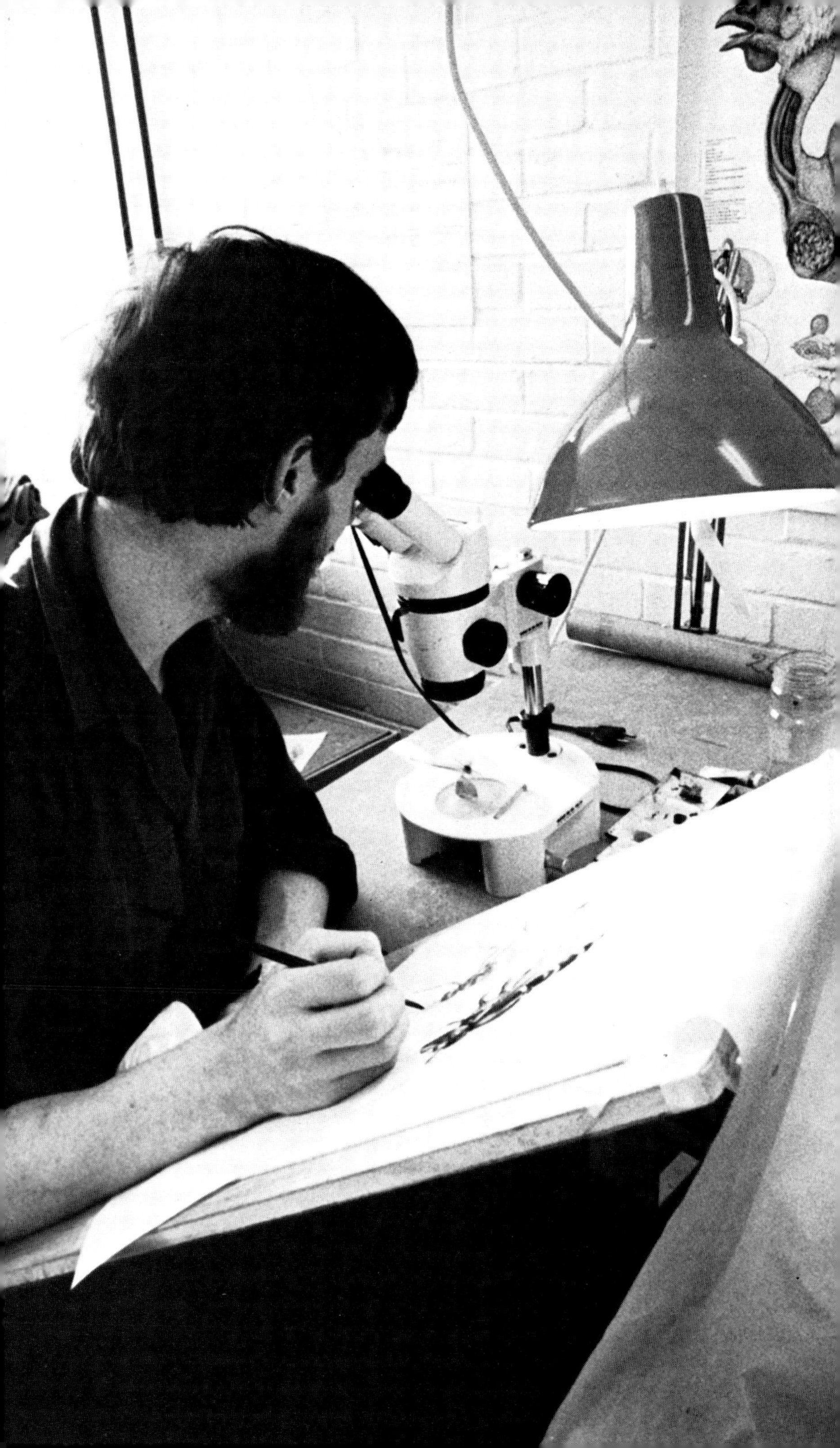

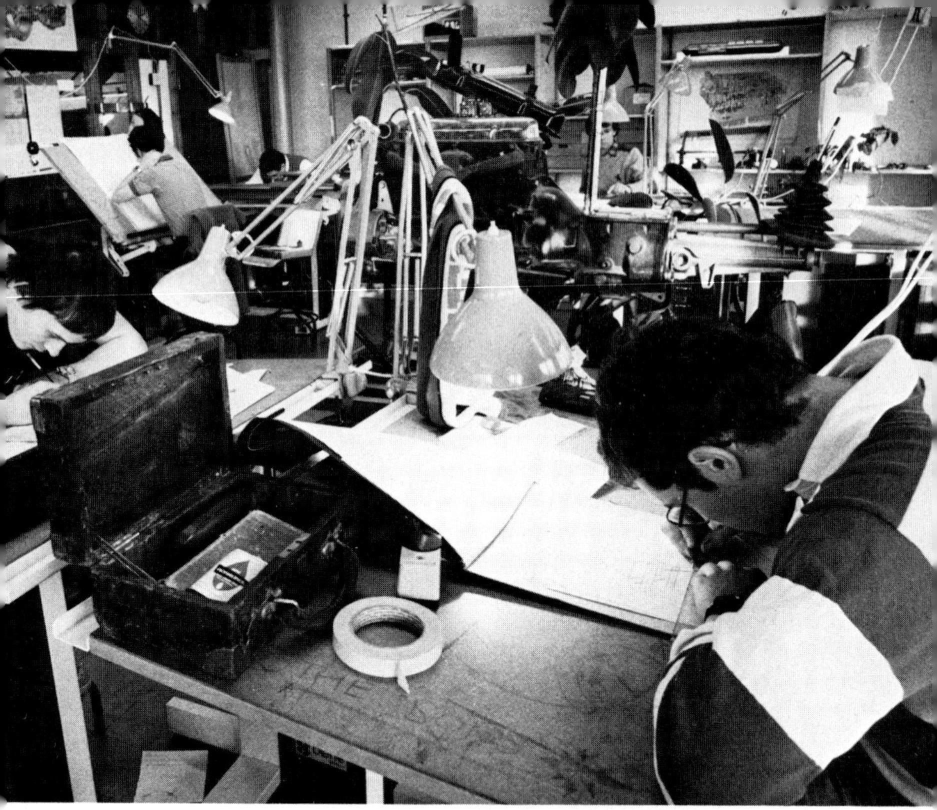

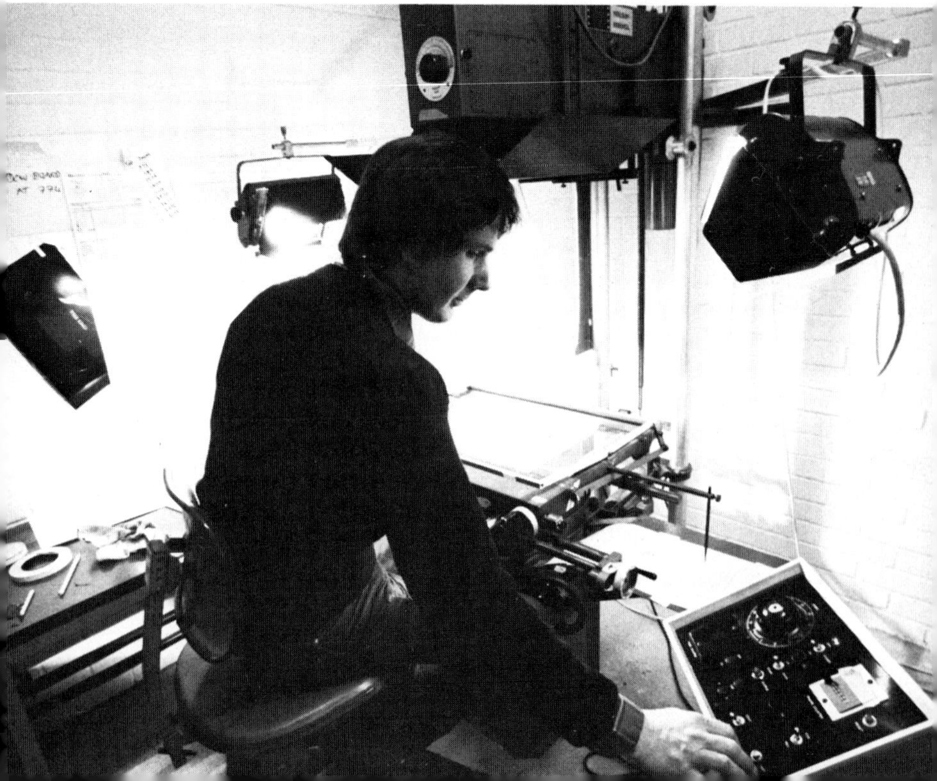

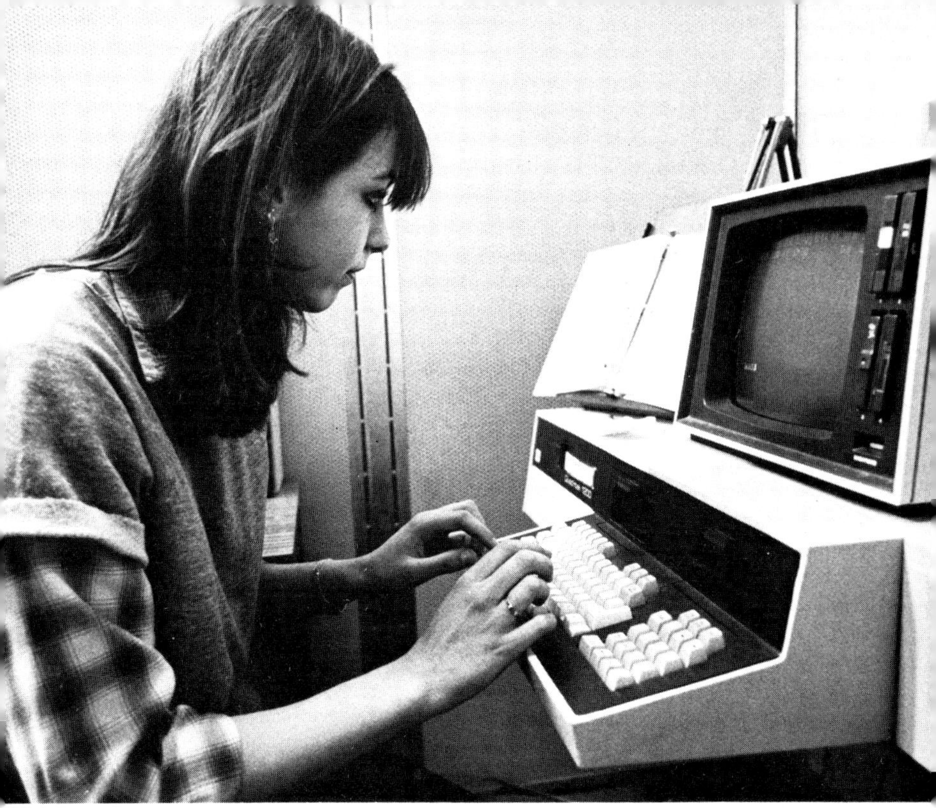

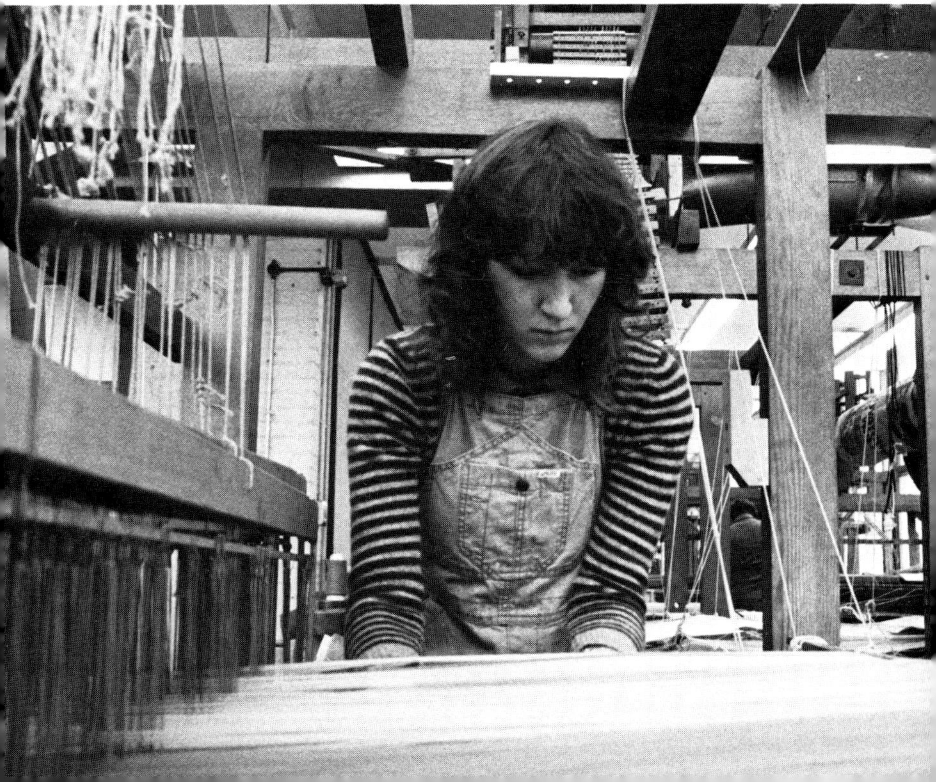

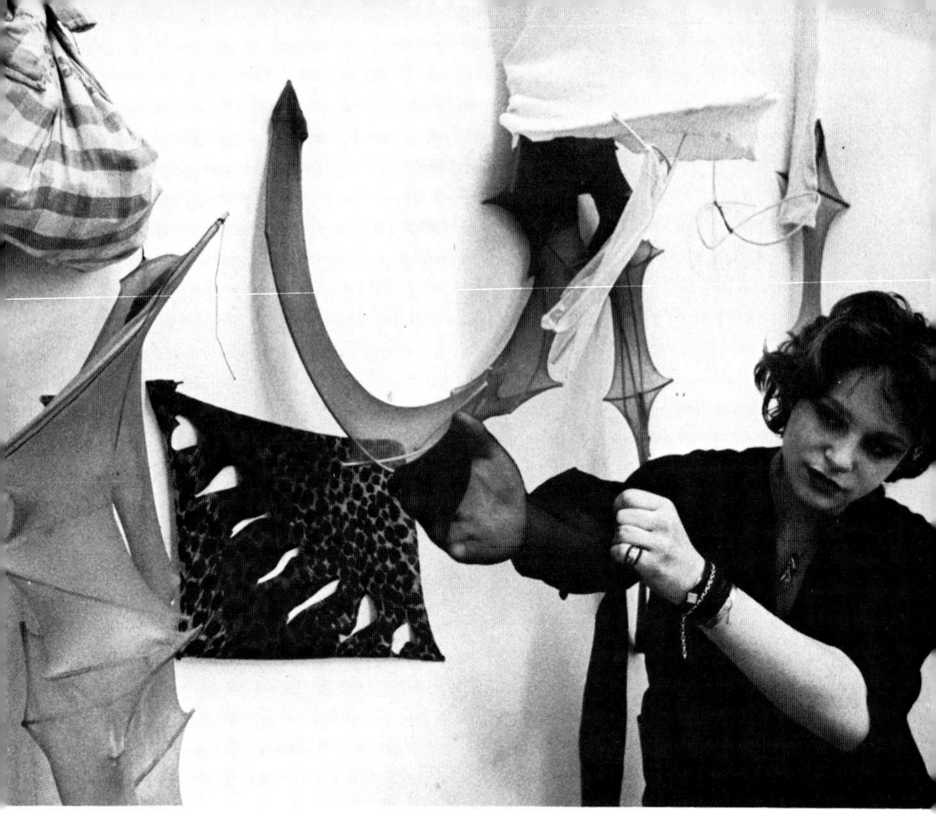

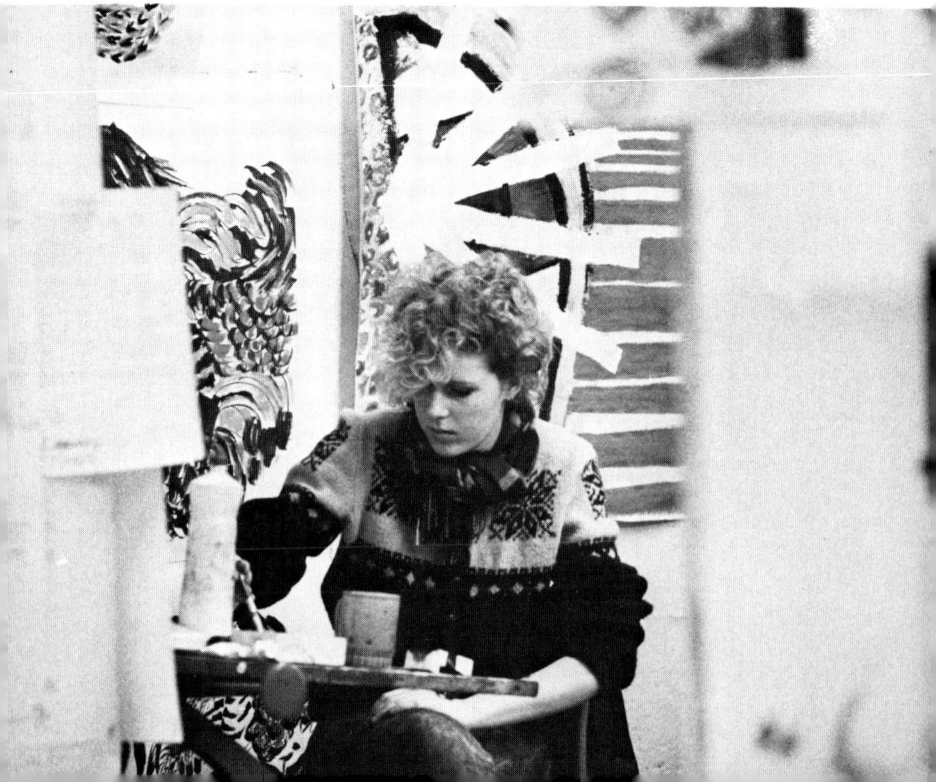

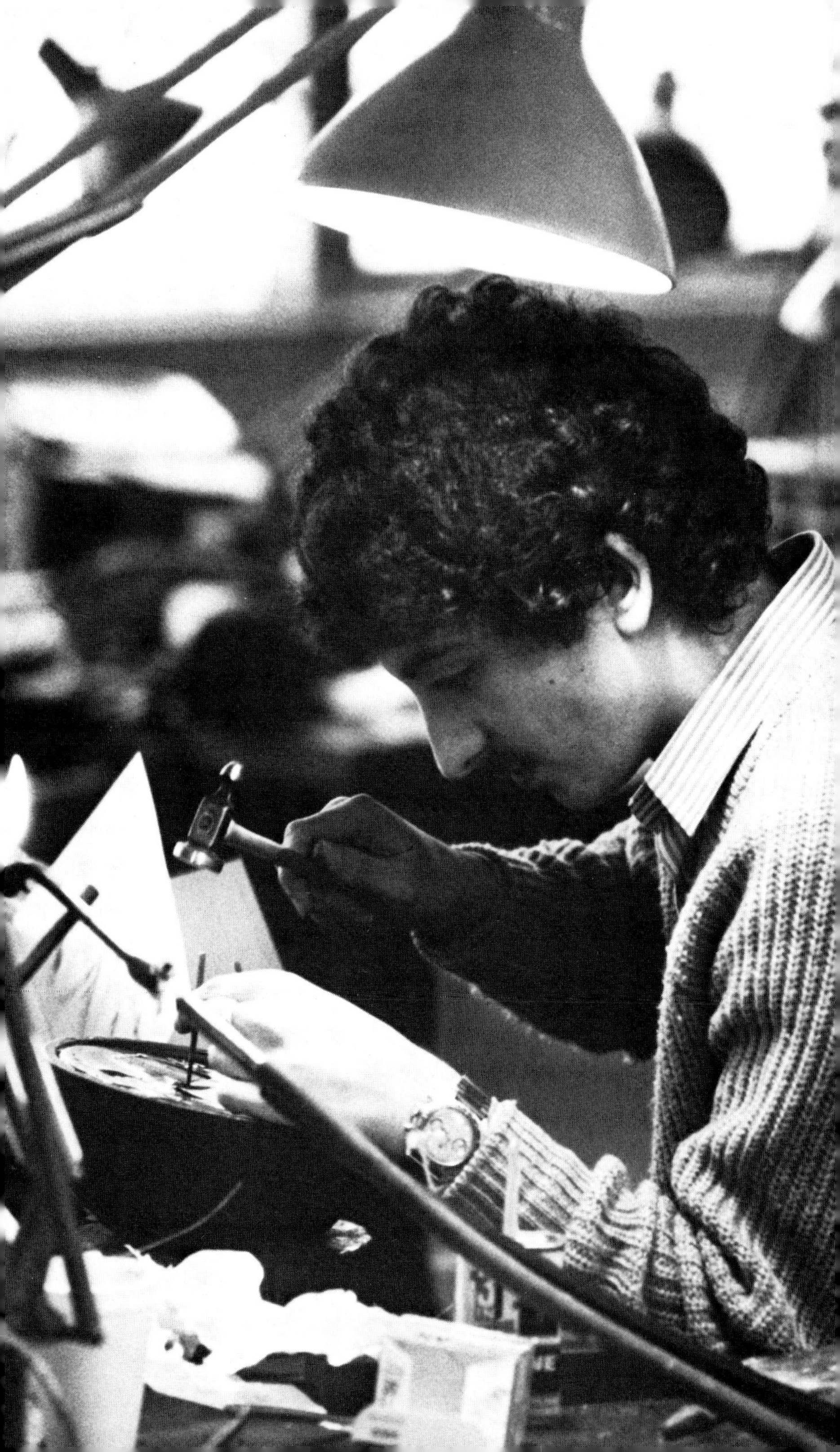

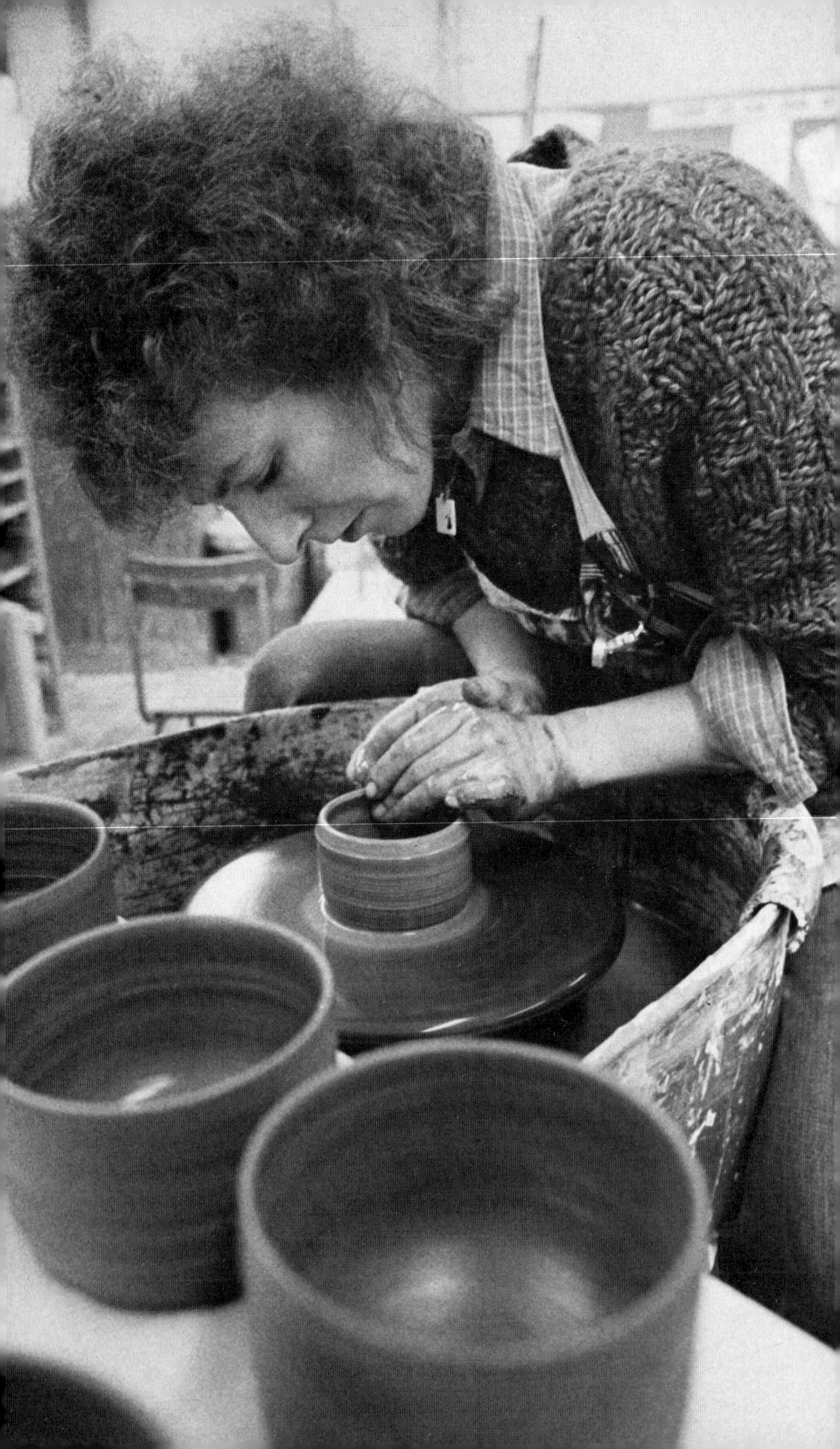

Some specific occupations—a broad guide

ability particularly in the basic skills of layout, drawing, typography and photography.

The major areas of work are found in the following occupations and categories of graphic design.

(i) Advertising and publicity design—Advertising art director

Advertising is probably the largest single employer of graphic designers. Within an advertising agency all the graphic skills are used, normally under the control of an art director. A young designer, starting in a large advertising agency, will probably become a junior member of the art group. At the beginning of his career he will possibly be restricted to basic graphic tasks related to layout and art work preparation, but as he or she progresses more sophisticated design talents will be required, such as objectivity and reasoning in design and taking part in the decision making processes of the group.

The essential role of the art director in an advertising agency is to create ideas and coordinate the work of a group of graphic artists and designers. In co-operation with the copy writer it is his or her job to think of new ideas and themes which will apeal to the public, and meet the client's requirements. Working with the account executive and the copy writer, the art director plays an important part in the major decisions on any project or campaign. After the general approach for any project has been established, the art director consults with his group of designers, co-ordinates the work of the agency designers and usually is the person who consults with the client and discusses ideas with him as they are produced.

The graphic design work going through any advertising agency is normally infinitely varied and usually the members of the art group have specialist skills and abilities which are used for various aspects of the work—for example, one designer may specialise in packaging while another would be more concerned with typography or illustration. Though all members of the group require a basic knowledge of, for example, layout, illustration, typography and photography.

The art director therefore normally co-ordinates the work of the art group, is responsible for the basic original idea and liaises with the Board of Directors and the client. The art director is usually also responsible for working with the printers or production department to ensure not only that the design can be produced adequately but also that they can be produced within the budget allocated to any programme.

Advertising agencies obviously vary in their size and the number of people they employ. The tendency is for work in the larger agencies to be divided up into single specialist jobs for each

Some specific occupations — a broad guide

individual designer; while smaller agencies obviously require the designer to work across a number of different graphic design disciplines. The primary work of an advertising agency is concerned with the visualisation of ideas, the layout of words and images and the preparation of the artwork for printing production. Specialist artwork, illustration or photography is sometimes contracted out to freelance artists.

(ii) Art editor — magazine and book publishing

The job of the art editor (or art director) for a magazine or book publisher is, in many respects, similar to that of the art director in an advertising agency. A magazine art editor for example has to work closely with editors and sub-editors, printers, freelance artists and assistant graphic designers working for him or her.

An art editor normally heads a team of graphic artists and designers and is responsible for allocating work to the team. The art editor, in simple terms, discusses the overall possible appearance of a magazine with the chief editor. The balance between advertising material and editorial copy, the look of the magazine, what needs illustrations, what lettering and type to use, how much space to allocate to pictures — all has to be discussed. When these basic decisions have been taken with the editor, the work is passed to assistant designers, or undertaken by the art editor — depending on the size of the graphic design department and magazine. The editor and art editor therefore decide on the overall policy for the visual appearance of the magazine or book and the next stage is to allocate layout and artwork to assistant designers. Rather like the advertising art director, the art editor is responsible for consulting with the printers and production departments and also commissions work from freelance artists. In addition an art editor is responsible for the overall appearance of a magazine or book.

Book publishing is obviously rather different from magazine production in a number of ways. Magazines appear regularly and at short intervals, every week or month, and magazines carry advertising material which has to be incorporated into the overall appearance of the magazine. Art editors in book publishing are responsible for the overall design and layout of the book, the type size and page layout, and for commissioning any illustrations. In addition, the book cover or jacket has to be designed. Depending on the size of the publishing company this work is either undertaken by the art editor, acting as graphic designer, illustrator, jacket designer and layout artist, all in one, or passed to assistant designers or sent out as commissions to freelance artists. Art editors, in short, are responsible for the overall visual

Some specific occupations—a broad guide

production of whatever is published, with the specialised graphic design work either produced by assistant designers or freelance artists.

(iii) General illustration—books and magazines
Illustrators either work as freelance artists or in commercial studios. Art editors or art directors, as we have seen, normally commission illustrations from artists working in commercial studios, or from individual freelance artists, working at home.

Book and magazine illustration are only part of the varied demand for illustrative material. Advertising material needs art work, book jackets and record sleeves need drawings and even packaging often includes drawings or pictoral material—to say nothing of the whole range of technical, instructional and scientific illustration used in diagrams, maps, plans, leaflets or textbooks.

The art editor of the book or magazine, or art director of the advertising agency—being responsible for the overall design, indicates to the artist the space available for illustration, which determines the size of the picture. The artist must read the story or article he has to illustrate and normally discusses ideas or rough drawings with the art editor, or sometimes even with the author of the book. Unless the artist's work is very well known to the art editor, the illustrator may be asked to submit rough sketches for approval. This sometimes may cause difficulties if his idea is rejected. When a freelance commissioned artist's work is rejected the artist is normally entitled to a rejection fee. But not all companies respect this agreement and it is one of the risks a freelance artist has to work with. An illustrator working in a commercial studio, on the other hand, is of course paid a salary or wage for whatever work he or she undertakes. The studio artist however has no choice in what he has to illustrate though work related to any specific skill or interest may be given to him. The freelance illustrator has the advantage of choosing what work to accept, but has all the other difficulties associated with being self-employed and waiting for commissions. As we already know, getting started as a freelance artist on your own, provides little choice of commissions to begin with, and artists are wise to accept initially any job that comes their way. Once a few illustrations have been published the freelance artist may gradually begin to exercise some selection about jobs, in trying to build up a special reputation. Most freelance illustrators employ an agent, who gets work for the artist, but naturally takes a commission on all fees paid.

Some specific occupations—a broad guide

A major area for book illustration work is in the field of children's books, which obviously use more pictures, but as we have seen illustrations or pictorial material are used, in combination with words, in nearly everything which is printed or published.

(iv) Technical, scientific and medical illustration
Book and magazine illustrators primarily interpret a story, or decorate a page, adding colour, visual interest and impact to the publication. Technical illustrators, on the other hand, have a different job to do, their responsibility is to convey information clearly and precisely. There is a great demand for technical illustration in textbooks, instructional leaflets, diagrams, mechanical and technical manuals, educational books and information sheets.

The technical illustrator produces precision drawings showing exactly how something works or fits together. Technical illustrators are employed by educational publishers, research departments in industry, government information departments, the manufacturing industries and advertising and publicity agencies. The technical illustrator's job is therefore to convey information accurately so that complex machinery, or production processes, or information and statistics, can be understood clearly. Techncial illustrators must have a sound knowledge of drawing methods, including the various techniques of perspective and cut away drawings, showing the internal workings of machines or mechanical parts. The illustrator must also 'design' a drawing, in that he, or she, must find the most appropriate visual method of communicating the information, whatever form this may take. There is a difference therefore between a draughtsman—who basically draws up and makes plans (usually working with a designer, engineer or architect)—and a technical illustrator whose job is to design the most effective way to communicate information visually.

Technical illustration is not just about conveying mechanical or technical information—though this is obviously a large part of the work—it also includes scientific and medical illustration, and any work related to information design. For example, the illustration of any book or publication about botany, zoology, wild life, nature study, biology, in fact any encyclopaedia, text book or instructional publication, uses the work of the technical illustrator.

While technical and scientific illustrators are usually employed by industry, government departments or specialist publishers (on a full-time or freelance basis), medical illustrators usually work in large hospitals. Medical illustration is a very specialised area of the

Some specific occupations—a broad guide

visual communication industry and the large teaching hospitals need medical illustrators as part of their teaching and research programmes. The work of the technical illustrator is gradually, in part, being effected by the use of computers. Graphic designers and visual communicators are now trained in the use of computers and some aspects of information graphics are now being covered by computer graphics in which the designer uses the computer as a tool in communicating the necessary information accurately.

(v) Model making
A familiar part of work in technical graphics is the use of models. Graphic designers frequently make considerable use of models to either illustrate a theme, or convey information in three-dimensional form. The completed model is then photographed and used in conjunction with type as part of the art work for production.

Many graphic designers will have done some model making while a student and may well therefore construct the model themselves. The designer however is usually more likely to pass this work either to a specialist model maker, working in the design agency, or send the work out to a model making agency or freelance model maker.

(vi) The typographer
Typography is an essential ingredient in all graphic design work for it is basically about the use of type—it is part of advertising, packaging, sign making, television graphics and all book and magazine production. Because typography relates closely to all graphic production processes, it is normally undertaken in the design studio or agency and not sent out for freelance work. Typographers therefore normally work as staff designers, in design offices, responsible for the layout, size and arrangement of all the lettering.

In display work or advertising the 'copy' (that is the words to be used) are discussed by the typographer with the art director. The typographer has first to choose the most suitable type face for the particular job. There are thousands of different type faces from which to choose and you have to choose one that helps get the message over effectively. Having selected a suitable type face, the size and arrangement of the letters has to be decided—and an overall 'layout' carefully considered. The skill of the typographic designer is of course to ensure that the information is conveyed with the maximum clarity and legibility, and that the type layout communicates the idea efficiently, and appropriately relates with any visual material.

Some specific occupations—a broad guide

The typographer's job includes 'marking up' the copy for the typesetter—this means giving clear instructions to the printer or typesetter. This work requires that the typographer is familiar with all the letter generating processes, ranging from hand type setting through to film setting and computer type setting.

The typesetter usually then returns the printed matter in 'proof', or printed form, which is then pasted down, along with any illustrations, to form the complete 'art work'. This is then normally photographed and transferred onto a printing block, plate or screen. The pasting down or arranging of all the visual elements—words and pictures—is usually the work of 'paste-up' or 'layout' artists.

(vii) Layout artists

Layout artists are often junior assistant graphic designers whose job is to 'lay out' or arrange, on white card, the various elements of words and pictures. In book production this may mean 'laying out' or arranging, to a previously designed and agreed grid, the printed proofs of the type, and fitting in any illustrations or pictures according to the designer's instructions. A paste-up has to be made for every page, so in a large book this can be repetitive. Paste-up work for other printed material such as advertising or display work, or magazine production is naturally much more varied.

If a junior assistant, the layout artist will work to a designer's or art editor's instructions, though frequently senior designers may combine the work of typographer, designer and layout artist. Layout and paste-up work is however most commonly undertaken by young designers starting work in a studio or design office. To gain experience many college leavers must expect to start work in a studio as paste-up and layout artists; graduating with experience to some of the more demanding work. If however you are both designing the layout and pasting it down, then the work takes on a different character.

(viii) The sign designer

An area of work associated with graphic design, but not the printing industry, is the production of signs and notices. Signs and notices, or the public display of information, can take many forms—shop lettering, road signs and illuminated signs; in fact any form of public notice whether in the street, on vans or lorries, or at railways stations, museums or airports. the large scale use of acrylic sheeting, screen printed transfer lettering and illumination has revolutionised the sign industry.

Some specific occupations—a broad guide

Formally all this work was undertaken by the craftsman signwriter—we still sometimes see him at work (and a few openings for work and training still exist)—but today screen printing, and plastic sheet lettering and illuminations have largely taken over.

The so-called sign industry basically falls into three categories: the small firm dealing possibly with sign writing and general silk screen printing; the medium sized firm producing acrylic lettering with possibly some illumination, and more complex screen printing; and lastly the large company undertaking electrical advertising and sophisticated lettering in stainless steel or any other material.

The small firm requires craft skills in lettering and screen printing and some graphic designers may in fact set up small businesses of their own to do this work. The medium sized firms may probably employ two or three designers whose work may include enlarging type faces for the letter cutters to produce stencils for silkscreen work. They may also need to produce original designs for a wide variety of work, and this may be undertaken on a freelance basis. The really large companies will normally have a design studio, employing designers under the supervision of a studio manager. The sign designer needs to have a knowledge of lettering and typography and be able to draw lettering and understand design principles. He may also, in some cases, require a basic knowledge of building construction and be able to produce highly finished technical drawing, and to have a working knowledge of the materials and techniques used in sign production, including metals, plastics, screen printing and the technology of electrical illuminations.

(ix) Packaging design
Nearly everything we buy, from perfume to butter, is wrapped and packaged. The visual appearance of the package helps sell the product, as well as containing and protecting it. Packaging therefore not only contains a product but is a form of advertising and brand image promotion, and as such is a major part of the graphic design industry. The design of packaging therefore has close connections with advertising. Many advertising agencies carry out this work, which is also sometimes undertaken in the design departments of large manufacturing firms or by consultant freelance designers.

Designing wrapping paper is a straightforward two-dimensional graphic design job, but package design basically combines elements of product design with graphics. The designer, as well as dealing with the graphics printed on the package, must also know

Some specific occupations — a broad guide

whether the constructed package will hold the contents properly. He must know the physical nature of the product—its size, shape and weight and whether it is a paste, powder, solid or liquid. There is clearly a wide range of materials from which the package may be made including metals, plastic, glass, cardboard, paper. The designer must therefore have a working knowledge of these materials and how they can be formed to give strength, air-tightness, water-tightness, and how they can be decorated or shaped or printed on. The work also includes the need to know about printing inks and surfaces and the way in which containers can be filled, labelled, stoppered, opened or poured from. All this calls for a combination of graphic designer and industrial product designer.

A knowledge of marketing and merchandising techniques is also necessary as a package is normally part of a manufacturer's overall marketing campaign, fitting in with other display, advertising and product presentation. Packaging usually also has to carry important information about the product so the design must include the work of the typographer. The complex nature of package design usually requires the work to be undertaken in a design studio, where a range of skills are available, or in a design consultancy, with specialist aspects of the work sent out to freelance designers.

(x) Work as a photographer

Work as a photographer covers an extremely wide variety of activities—it is a confusing field as nearly every aspect of work in art and design uses photography in some form or another.

Photography is obviously used a great deal in graphic design—in fact it is, in one sense, a basic tool for all designers. Specialist photographers are used for artwork and illustrative material in all forms of graphic design, and art editors and designers normally commission professional photographers to produce finished artwork when required. Some design agencies employ their own photographer but the majority of specialist photography, used by graphic designers or advertising agencies, is commissioned, on a freelance basis, from professional photographers.

Although graphic designers are trained in the use of photography, and may produce work for production, most photographers are trained specialists—having either taken a specialist course in photography (such as a degree course in photography or the Incorporated Photographer's examination or a City and Guilds qualification) or learnt their craft through in-service training. That is, started work as a trainee or studio assistant while attending college on a part-time evening or day

Some specific occupations—a broad guide

release basis.

In simple terms there are four main areas of work for photographers, outside the everyday use that designers and artists make of photography. Firstly the industrial use of process photography, as in the printing industry, where photography is used as part of the technical process of making negatives for the production of printing blocks, screens and plates. Secondly, there is the large area of what can be described as technical photography. This would include the specialist fields of architectural and medical photography and work within the service branches, such as the police, post office, and Civil Service Commission. In this area the particular industries frequently train photographers for use in their specific field.

Thirdly, by far the largest field of photographic work is what can be described as creative photography, usually undertaken by small agencies and studios. Such studios usually operate on a freelance contractual basis and are made up of the photographer, with possibly a technician or trainee learning the basic trade. Such small studios are set up either by graphic designers, who have specialised in photography, or more often by specialist photographers, either trained at college, or who learnt their trade by persuading a professional to take them on as a usually unpaid assistant.

Finally, there is the fourth field of photographic journalism. This requires the normal journalists ticket and frequently the trade is learnt by working one's way up through small commissions or local paper work. Few opportunities exist in this field and competition for work is difficult.

(xi) Film animation

Work as an animator for television or film is part of the graphic designer's work. Animation techniques are used extensively in advertising and are also employed in the production of television credits.

A graphic designer, working as an animator, is likely to work in one of three places. If in advertising the designer would most probably work at an advertising agency, as many agencies employ their own film animators.

Secondly, if working on television credits the designer would normally work in the design studios of the television company, though some work is sent out to specialist agencies.

Thirdly, some small companies specialise in making animated films for advertising companies, television bodies or film companies, and the designer could be employed by such an organisation.

Some specific occupations—a broad guide

Animation is an art based largely on drawings or images which must, when photographed, produce the illusion of movement. There are 25 images or drawings for every second of animated film on a television screen, giving some idea of the amount of work needed for every film. Because of the amount of work involved teams of designers and technicians usually work together on any production, with the work divided into separate parts. Normally when the story or sequence has been established the layout department produce a series of drawings showing the stage by stage development (this is called the story board). The backgrounds are usually produced by different artists to those producing the animated characters. Teams of animators normally draw up the many stages required for each shot and 'tracers' rather than artists or designers, often transfer drawings to celluloid sheets and 'painters' colour them in. In small agencies or studios the designer or artists may do much of the repetitive work himself, while in larger groups there is scope for the designer to work alongside technicians and what are, in effect, technical draughtsmen.

Animators may of course use models and cut outs, and montage techniques, all of which can be used to create illusions of movement. Many different techniques exist and graphic designers often do their own film making, as animation basically combines the skills of drawing, layout, photography and film making, which most designers have experience of. Film animation is an integral part of most graphic designer's training and plays a significant part in both television, graphics and advertising.

(xii) Film making

Entry to the production side of the film industry remains very difficult indeed. However, the use of film techniques is increasing, particularly in the field of educational graphics and opportunities for trainees do occur from time to time. Formal training is normally required and those entering the industry often find initial jobs to be rather humble. In addition to college based training, limited occasional opportunities occur through the BBC film trainee scheme. Most graphic design courses include some work in film making, as an extension to photography, and graphic designers may well work in close association with film makers, particularly small film units and agencies producing advertising films. Professional film making is however a complex industry requiring a team of specialists including, cameramen, producers, directors, lighting experts, editors and sound recordists.

The film industry has many branches, ranging from feature film

Some specific occupations — a broad guide

production to instructional and educational films, and including advertising and television films. The most likely areas for initial jobs are in the field of educational film making and advertising work. Film makers and designers with experience and training in film making, and audio-visual techniques, may more easily find work in these smaller production units than in the difficult world of the major film companies. Formal professional training is however necessary, either at graduate or post-graduate level.

(xiii) Television graphics

Much of what we see on television is the work of a graphic designer. The title and logo designs for all programmes, together with the front and end credits; the announcements and trailers for future programmes; and all visual inserts in programmes such as diagrams, charts, illustrations and animated sequences are all prepared by graphic designers.

Most television graphic designers are employed by the BBC or commercial companies (in fact the BBC Graphics Department is one of the largest in the country), though some work is prepared by specialist agencies.

It is necessary for the television designer to combine designing skills with film techniques and frequently to present a mass of information in a few seconds of screen time. The work is varied and interesting but the tempo of production can be fast, and the designer has to work under pressure, with items for news programmes and current affairs produced at the shortest notice.

Much of the work may include standard graphic design activities such as layout and typography, but animation or live action calls for additional knowledge in film techniques. Normally young designers start with layout and typographic work for credits and with experience gradually move on to film work, animation and the many other techniques through which graphic images can be produced. New technology is certainly affecting television design and designers need to be able to learn and adapt to new production methods. The computer has, for example, recently made a considerable impact in the production of television graphics. Designers must therefore work closely with technicians and be prepared to keep themselves fully up to date with new and changing technical processes.

The film industry also offers opportunities for graphic designers, though in feature films the graphic designer's work is usually limited to the preparation of titles and credits. Advertising films for television and the cinema however offer a greater amount of work for the graphic designer. These films are made by film

Some specific occupations — a broad guide

companies specialising in advertising and their graphic designers usually work to a rough layout, prepared by the advertising agency commissioning the film — though sometimes the film company has its own advertising studio and designers.

(xiv) Visual aids for education — educational graphics
We have already seen how educational publishing, text books and children's books provide much work for the graphic designer. A further growing part of this industry, for the graphic designer, is the preparation of visual and audio-visual aids for educational and instructional purposes. There is a wide range of teaching aids in use, from teaching machines, pictorial wall charts, together with projected aids such as film strips, film loops, overhead projectors and slide-tape programmes. Graphic designers working in this field will be selecting and designing captions, preparing photographs, designing animation sequences, and preparing sets of slides and overlays for the overhead projector. Information for education and training has to be concise, and accurate, with the visual and verbal message conveyed in a lively way. Employment may be found with commercial organisations who actually produce visual aids and kits, though the film making is often sent out to specialist agencies.

In addition to specialist companies producing educational material, some large educational authorities employ their own designers to produce educational graphics and audio-visual aids. Educational television and broadcasting also includes follow-up pamphlets, teachers' notes and film strips and educational graphics can, therefore, form a large part of the work of a television graphics department. Many large commercial companies issue their own instructional, educational and public relations material, for loan to schools and colleges, normally in the form of films, wallcharts or booklets. This work is either undertaken by the company's graphic designers or, more frequently, sent out to freelance designers or specialist educational graphic design agencies or firms.

(xv) Lettering, calligraphy and bookbinding
Bookbinding and lettering are two traditional hand crafts which have become almost totally mechanised. Graphic designers still require a working knowledge of lettering and letter forms and the book and magazine designer needs to understand how books are bound — but generally we no longer do these jobs ourselves.

There are however still some bookbinders and calligraphers, working as craftsmen-designers. Hand craft bookbinders now normally produce limited editions of fine bindings for presentation or sale in craft exhibitions, or in response to individual

Some specific occupations—a broad guide

commissions. Opportunities for work as a craft bookbinder are however provided in the field of conservation (see paper conversation page 135). Large libraries and museums employ craft bookbinders who are highly skilled in the repairing and conservation of books and documents.

Calligraphers, by which we normally mean pen-letterers, and hand lettering artists, now mainly work as craftsmen-designers taking on freelance commissions for presentation documents, commemorative books, illuminated addresses, and decorative maps and charts. A few specialist courses in calligraphy are still offered (such as at Redhill/Reigate School of Art) and these sometimes include aspects related to heraldry, and heraldic illumination, which is part of the traditional calligrapher's work. Hand lettering can still play a part in the graphic designer's work, both in terms of rough visualisation of a layout, and in producing original letter forms not found within the range of normal typefaces. Lettering artists also have a role to play in the sign producing industry (see page 102).

2 Three-dimensional design

As you will have already discovered, three-dimensional design includes a mass of different articles ranging from small hand made objects to large industrial design products. Three-dimensional design therefore operates through a complex mixture of small traditional craft industries and large mass production manufacturers.

We have already looked at the difference between a craftsman designer working on his own, or in a small business, and the staff designer employed full-time as part of a design production team in industry. Work in three-dimensional design covers this entire range.

(i) The traditional industrial crafts

By traditional industrial crafts is meant those materials and processes which, although now industrialised, have a long hand craft tradition. These crafts would include, for example, silverware, jewellery, glassware, china or ceramics and furniture. All these crafts now have industrial production structures, but work for the designer-craftsman also continues.

In simple, and rather generalised terms, there is what may be described as a three-tier structure within the industrial crafts.
1 Designer-craftsmen and women producing items by hand.
2 Small factories and workshops using some machinery, and a

Some specific occupations—a broad guide

certain amount of handicraft, in which the designer-craftsman both makes 'one-offs' and designs for limited production.

3 Large manufacturing industries and companies using mass-production methods to produce thousands of articles exactly alike. Such factories usually employ staff designers as part of a production team.

As has been explained in an earlier chapter the big manufacturers usually employ staff designers, while smaller firms may employ staff for design work or alternatively commission freelance designers. In both cases the functions of design and manufacture are separate. The designer-craftsman, as we know, carries out his own design, sometimes with help from assistants, and unlike the designer for factory production, he has direct contact with the purchaser and is responsible for the complete making process. Hand craft methods, as we have seen, are more expensive than machine production and the designer-craftsman usually caters for customers who want articles of an individual or special nature. None of the traditional craft industries offer many openings and successful designers frequently operate both as a freelance designer for industry and as a craftsman-designer.

(ii) Silverware

Silver (like gold) is an expensive material and this therefore limits demand for silverware, and consequently the amount of work that exists for designers in this area—the craftsman goldsmith and silversmith have the same problem in that they are both working with a precious metal.

The mass-production side of the silverware industry uses silver plate and stainless steel both of which are considerably cheaper than silver. There is a substantial market for domestic cutlery, tableware, powder compacts, boxes, candlesticks, tankards and trophies all of which are mass-produced in factories usually sited in Sheffield or Birmingham. These large firms employ staff designers and much of the work is mechanically produced, though hand craft methods are still used for some of the decoration. As well as the market for mass-produced silver plate, and stainless steel ware, there is a demand for individual work. This may include, for example, commissions for silverware from churches or from public corporations, or from wealthy private clients. Freelance designers, designer-craftsmen, and the staff designers of smaller firms all may specialise in this kind of work. Large firms may also, from time to time, take on special individual commissions as their designers and craftsmen are as equally skilled as the freelance designer-craftsmen, and factory workmen often carry out the work for special commissions by hand, if necessary.

Some specific occupations—a broad guide

While the production industry is sited mainly in Sheffield or Birmingham, individual craftsmen-designers set up their workshops in London as this appears to be the most convenient siting for finding the commissions from commercial companies, and large organisations, who may require an expensive piece of silverware. Hand craftsmen or women working in silver clearly require to understand production methods, so that they can both work for industrially produced commissions and on hand made work.

(iii) Jewellery

As with all other traditional industrial crafts, jewellery has both a hand made sector and a mass-production industry covering a wide range of items from very expensive fine jewellery, through to cheap mass-produced costume jewellery.

There are not a great number of opportunities for staff designers in the jewellery industry. Companies producing the cheaper range of costume jewellery tend not to redesign their products, but purely modify existing models, and reproduce traditional designs; this work normally does not require a trained designer. The trained and skilled creative designer therefore either works as a freelance designer-craftsman or as a staff designer for what can be described as the 'upper ranges' of manufactured jewellery. Good costume jewellery, and that made with semi-precious stones, offers some scope for the designer. Sometimes this work is closely associated with the dress trade and a knowledge of fashion may be useful. This type of work is often undertaken by the smaller firms, where there are some opportunities for freelance designers and artist craftsmen.

One of the problems of designing for the industry is the anxiety that expensive and precious jewellery should not date or go out of fashion too quickly. This concern tends to influence manufacturers towards retaining traditional designs which may therefore restrict the opportunities for design work. From this it is evident that some of the best openings are found in the small workshops or for artists setting up on their own as freelance craftsmen-designers. Direct retail outlets for hand made jewellery are reasonably available, particularly in London and fashionable consumer market areas. Many young jewellery craftsmen sell their work from their workshops, or on market stalls, or at local craft shops and large stores and this in many senses is one of the best ways to start work as a craftsman-designer. Although the material used may be expensive, setting up as a craftsman-jeweller does not require much expensive plant or a large amount of space.

Some specific occupations—a broad guide

(iv) Glassware

Unlike the jeweller, the craftsman in glass, finds it difficult to set up in a small individual workshop as the cost of kilns, and the space needed, makes this difficult. Unless the glass designer can afford to set up his or her own workshop, most of the opportunities for work must be found as a freelance designer or staff designer for industry.

Mass-production processes are used to produce most glassware for everyday domestic use. Glass of this type is made either by blowing or pressing molten glass into metal moulds. The designer must therefore have a certain knowledge of basic engineering design in addition to his other skills. More expensive glass is produced by craftsmen blowing the glass and some scope for designers if found designing the decoration. Glass is decorated sometimes with coloured vitreous enamel designs and more traditionally by cutting, facetting or engraving. Craftsmen undertaking this work follow the designs and drawings of the designer, who must work closely with the craftsmen, and have a clear working knowledge of decorating techniques.

Clearly opportunities for designer-craftsmen are rather limited but there is at present, an increasing interest in studio glassware and more opportunities for designer-craftsmen to set up their own workshops are being found.

Where plastics has taken over, in part, the china and glassware industry, then opportunities do exist for staff designers to design plastic products for domestic and commercial tableware. Plastics is a new industry without a craft tradition and industrial designers are employed by companies, either on a freelance basis, or as staff designers, to design goods which may have previously been made in glass or china.

(v) Pottery-ceramics

The ceramics industry, really meaning all objects made of clay, whereas 'pottery' implies only pots, is a difficult industry to enter as a designer. There is a world of difference between the small studio pottery and the mass-production industry of ceramics. There are artist-craftsmen making and decorating pottery in small 'studio' craft potteries all over the country. These craft workshops produce both functional and decorative pottery and sometimes employ young apprentices or assistants who have just left college. Clearly this is one way of working as a potter, either setting up your own studio workshop or gaining employment as an assistant in a studio pottery. Artist-craftsmen follow the complete production process through themselves, including finding retail outlets for their work.

Some specific occupations—a broad guide

Industrial ceramic companies employ a limited number of assistant designers, direct from college (often a local college offering specialised training), but opportunities are not very numerous in industry and a newly appointed assistant designer is usually given practical experience in the industrial methods of shaping, firing, decorating and glazing before he or she undertakes any design work.

Some opportunities exist for designing the decoration to be placed on utensils, but much of this work is still based on traditional designs which may only occasionally be modified. The designs of mass-produced tableware are not altered very frequently and the demand for designers, particularly freelance artists, is therefore limited, though freelance work in designing decorative tiles and commemorative ceramics is more common. The division between craftsmen-designers and the mass-produced manufacture of ceramics is very strongly defined in the ceramics industry; more so than most. Openings for the college leaver therefore mainly occur in the area of the studio potter, working in a small workshop as a craftsman-designer.

(vi) Furniture
Large furniture manufacturers, using mass-production processes, producing thousands of pieces of furniture to the same design, tended, until fairly recently, to rely on traditional designs yielding a large volume of sales without altering the design. Firms tended traditionally to cater for long established tastes, involing little more than alterations and modifications to existing designs. The situation however has improved, and many of the large companies now employ professional design staff.

However, it is in the medium sized firms that the majority of designers are to be found. These smaller companies generally use hand and machine processes together, in varying degrees, and there appears to be a growing demand for their work. The medium sized firms usually cannot however afford a full-time staff designer and tend therefore to employ freelance designers or consultants.

Furniture designers must know the markets in which their work is to be sold but above all they must understand production processes and the materials from which furniture is made. Wood is still the predominant material, though designers must also have a thorough working knowledge of other materials such as plastics, glass, metal, foam rubbers and fabrics. The designer needs to know, in technical terms, what is possible for both hand and machine processes and he or she must be able to work with technical staff.

Some specific occupations—a broad guide

A limited amount of furniture is still made by hand, the work carried out by the designer himself, or a craftsman working under his supervision. Hand made furniture is obviously expensive and is usually made to order for a commissioning client. Such work is usually rather expensive and forms only part of the total production of furniture.

(vii) Work as an industrial or product designer

We have already discussed in broad principle how the industrial designer works and it would not be possible to list all the types of manufacturing industries which employ a designer. It would be helpful however to think of those industries which have no hand craft traditions and consider the designer's work in the field for example of electrical appliances, plastics, metal, vehicle design and general product design. Firms in all these industries employ designers either as staff designers, or on a freelance basis.

In trying to understand something of the industrial designer's work it may help to simply consider three types of designer for industry:
1 The industrial designer
2 The industrial designer (engineering)
3 The engineering designer

The industrial, or product designer, is primarily responsible for the appearance of the manufactured object and the users' requirements and its marketable potential in terms of style. The industrial designer does not have to be involved with how the appliance operates (if it has a mechanical or electrical function) he or she is solely concerned with appearance, shape, form, colour and surface treatment.

The industrial designer (engineering)—as classified by the Design Council, needs, on the other hand, not only to understand the aesthetic and functional properties of a product, he must also understand the engineering problems connected with its manufacture. He is however not expected to have the thorough technological knowledge that would be expected of an engineering designer.

An engineering designer, as the name implies, is a trained engineer whose work is concerned with the design of mechanical and engineering functions. He is not responsible for the outward appearance of the object, appliance or machine, but purely its efficient operation.

An extremely wide range of goods is mass-produced and the range of processes and materials used is equally large. The variety ranges from hand tools used in the home, garden, or at work to kitchen appliances, mixers, scales, refrigerators, cookers, washing

Some specific occupations—a broad guide

machines, vacuum cleaners, light fittings, heaters, radiators, gas and electric fires, telephones, televisions and radios. The work of designers also covers car bodies, cycles, aircraft interiors, hospital equipment, street lighting, petrol-pumps—the range is endless and, although the work may be different, the approach to the problem of design is much the same, whatever the product. Usually once the board of directors has decided on what is to be made, a consultation takes place between the director responsible, the engineering designer, the production engineer, possibly the executive accountant, and the senior industrial designer. The team discusses such points as how many articles are to be produced, from what materials, at what price, and for what kind of customer or market. The machine tools available will also be discussed and what new tools and materials may be needed. All these considerations influence the industrial designers' thinking, and he must have a sound understanding of all the issues discussed. The industrial designer is part of a team, and working in consultation with other specialists throughout the design process is an integral part of the design practice.

When the industrial designer has obtained all the relevant information he begins his exploratory creative work, usually with rough drawings. These he will probably discuss with technical staff, and even the sales executive, to obtain the customer's view and check that his ideas are practicable. The designer then prepares more detailed drawings, finally producing comprehensive perspective drawings showing the article from all angles. He may also make detailed drawings of working parts to make his idea clearer, and show how it will work.

When the drawings have been approved models of the product are usually made in wood, plaster, cardboard or other materials to check that his drawings work. Models and drawings go through many stages of testing, alteration and discussion until a highly finished model is approved, as a final prototype, which is the first step towards putting the article into production. Some designers make their own models and drawings, but others have assistants to do this or send the work out to specialist agencies.

In large design studios the senior staff designer is rather like the art director of an advertising agency or graphics studio. It is the senior industrial designer who discusses the idea with the directors and engineering designer, and produces probably the first idea and guides the project through. Younger, assistant designers, will usually carry out the drawings and make up the models and work out the detailing, under the co-ordinating supervision of the senior designer. When a student has qualified he or she generally spends several years working in industry as an assistant to a senior staff

Some specific occupations—a broad guide

designer or with a consultant designer, before seeking a post as a staff designer or considering setting up as a consultant.

Industrial designers usually work as staff designers, employed by a manufacturing company, or as freelance consultant designers, working for a variety of manufacturers of different products. Consultant designers often work together in partnership with the advantage that a range of specialists, such as an architect, engineer, and designer may work together in the same group practice.

(viii) Model-making and technical draughtmanship
Industrial designers are trained to have some ability and knowledge of model making and technical draughtmanship and may make their own models and undertake their own technical drawing. This work is more often however passed on to specialist draughtmen and model makers. Such specialists may work in a large design office or be employed by consultant designers on a freelance basis. Specialist firms of model makers exist, working for a wide range of designers and manufacturers.

Specialist training, distinct from that which a designer receives is provided for model makers and draughtsmen, though young industrial designers frequently find themselves undertaking this work when they first join a design studio or work for a consultant.

(ix) Design technicians
Alongside draughtsmen and model makers are to be found design technicians who form the third part of the support team working with industrial designers. Design technicians normally have a broad knowledge of production processes, together with experience in prototype preparation. Design technicians assist designers on technical problems and may combine some of both the model maker's and draughtman's skills. Technicians, model makers and draughtsmen are either trained at college or enter industry from school, on a training scheme, which usually includes day release study at college.

(x) The interior designer
The interior designer's field of operation is basically concerned with any interior space, whether this is a house, restaurant, shop, hospital, school, theatre, hotel, office or ocean going liner or yacht. The interior designer normally works closely with architects—in fact their work has certain points in common. The interior designer, for example, must have a knowledge of building technology and materials and be familiar with the same health and

Some specific occupations—a broad guide

safety, and local government regulations, which architects have to work within.

There is of course a difference between the work of the interior designer and the interior decorator. The interior designer is concerned with the whole design and structural arrangement of an interior, the organisation of space and its disposition, not just the surfaces, colours and fabrics used. Interior designers work in a number of ways. They may, like architects, be in private practice, setting up consultancies of various sizes, or work in association or partnership with an architect. Large architectural departments of local authorities, for example, usually employ interior designers in their offices and a large number are of course in private practice; with architects or individual clients commissioning work from them on a freelance basis.

Whatever the interior being designed the normal pattern of work begins with the interior designer discussing what is required with the client. Having decided what is to be done, and the cost restraints, and methods of working, he analyses the problem and prepares various solutions. Possible solutions in the form of drawings and preliminary models are discussed with the client who selects a final design. The interior designer, or assistants in his office, then prepare detailed drawings and specifications which are put out to tender. Once the tender has been accepted the designer programmes and oversees the work of the builders, contractors and craftsmen, and approves the accounts for payment.

A parallel can be no doubt seen between the interior designer consulting with clients and contractors and the art director in a graphics agency or senior industrial staff designer—all consult with the clients and contractors and are responsible for the design solutions and overseeing the work of a group, or team of assistants. Young interior designers, when qualified, usually work in the office of a consultant interior designer as an assistant, gaining experience. The assistant designer will carry out detailed drawings, possibly help with model making and perhaps have a small part of the design scheme to carry through to completion. All this is valuable experience leading up to the time when the assistant may become a partner in a group, or a senior designer, or freelance consultant.

The interior designer usually has full responsibility for the design of the entire interior. This means he or she must have knowledge of lighting schemes and fittings, constructional building methods, architectural form, heating, acoustics, plumbing and surface treatments; to say nothing of colour

Some specific occupations—a broad guide

schemes, fabrics, furniture, floor coverings, fittings and all the elements that go to make up an interior. The designer and his assistants must be capable of drawing up professional plans, as projects often include building and structural work. As with other areas of design practice, models and the drawing of plans may either be undertaken by the designer, or his assistants, or passed over to the specialist model maker or architectural draughtsmen.

(xi) Interior decoration

Interior decoration, in broad terms, varies from interior design in that the decorator is only concerned with colour schemes, wall finishes, carpets, curtains and furnishing. The interior decorator is therefore not designing a total interior environment but advising on colour and decorative schemes. Interior decorators do not require the rigorous training, associated with the architectural and building industries, that the interior designer has to undergo.

Interior decorators usually have showrooms which stock examples of accessories and will expect to supply the client with most of these items. Consultant decorators need to be articulate and talk authoritatively about colour and current trends in furnishing and decoration. An ability to sketch and put down ideas, and a sense of colour, are essential but more detailed drawings or perspective are usually carried out by specialist freelance artists or draughtsmen. Some firms however may have their own studios where designers and draughtsmen interpret, in detail, the schemes the interior decorator has discussed and agreed with the client.

(xii) Exhibition designer

Exhibitions play an important part in the commercial, industrial, educational and cultural life of the country. Exhibitions are an essential part of promoting industry and communicating ideas and information. Designers of exhibitions may be architects, interior designers or specialists in exhibition design. Exhibition designers may work in group practices, or design offices, or be part of interior design or architectural practices. Some designers specialise in exhibition design, while others include the work along with other interior design work.

The demand for exhibition design is extensive and expanding and new ideas and solutions to problems are constantly being required. One of the reasons for the demand for work in this area is that exhibitions are usually not permanent, they are pulled down when the exhibition ends, so there is a constant need for new work. The designer normally starts with a plan of the site and must know exactly what is available in terms of lighting, heating, and

Some specific occupations—a broad guide

other services. He must design not just the display system but the entire structure and arrangement, controlling as it does the flow and movement of the public around the show. Exhibition design therefore combines display techniques with constructional, environmental and communication methods, together with lighting and basic promotional strategies. Planning an individual stand is obviously different from planning an entire exhibition, but demonstrates the possible range of the designer's work.

The designer normally submits rough sketches to the exhibitor for approval and then draws up detailed plans and a scale model. The designer is responsible for contracting the constructional work and supervising all the various craftsmen and electricians on site; he normally is in charge of the budget for the production and usually for hiring and furniture or fittings. In addition to working to a budget (like all designers) the designer is usually working to a tight time schedule, as irrespective of any of the difficulties the exhibition must open on time.

As with other areas, young designers normally work initially as assistants to exhibition designers producing drawings, plans or models and assisting in detailed preparation of various aspects of the work.

(xiii) Display design
Outlets for display design are mainly focused on the retail trade in terms of shop window display. Window displays have to be changed frequently providing a considerable demand for work. Display artists or designers can work in a number of ways. Small shops, for example, may use a freelance designer who travels around doing windows for a number of shops or, alternatively, a store may have its own display designer. Large stores may have a team of display assistants working under a senior display designer, who plans the total scheme for the store or its branches. Some large firms train their own display staff releasing them for part-time college based studies, while other display staff undertake full-time college training before taking up a post. Some senior display experts act as consultants drawing up schemes on a freelance basis for large stores. The schemes and ideas are then put into practice by the shop's own display staff.

(xiv) Theatre design—film and television set designer
While there are obvious similarities in designing for the theatre, films or television each has its own particular requirements and problems.

Theatre design The designer for the theatre is clearly limited by

Some specific occupations—a broad guide

the size and character of the particular stage for which he is designing. He will have to work to a scale drawing of the stage—though real problems occur if the play has to tour, or may transfer to another theatre. Designs are produced first as models and scale drawings and these are discussed at every stage with the actors and actresses, producer and the director. The designer must of course read, understand and absorb the nature of the play. He may well need to research historical and architectural detail and more than anything else ensure that his plan works both visually for the audience and practically, in terms of movement, for the actors.

Although some designers do not paint the scenery, many, especially those employed in repertory companies or small theatres, have to do so. After an art school training most designers start as assistants in theatre studios or with repertory companies. In this way they become involved in all sorts of work, including painting the scenery, making and painting props, and helping with the costumes and lighting. During this time valuable working experience is gained which may well lead to the opportunity to eventually design a production.

The film set designer works on a different and a varying scale compared with the restraints of the theatre stage. Work may be on interior sets or exterior location and include massive building projects or small scale models. The designer for film work is usually called an art director. Settings for the cinema normally demand more realism than the theatre, as they may be filmed at close range. The art director has a team working under him to undertake much of the detailed work. One of the assistants will usually be a chief draughtsman overseeing the drawing office where scale and working drawings will be produced and models made. The chief draughtsman may also be in charge of the many craftsmen, carpenters, painters and plasterers who build and decorate the sets. Another assistant is usually responsible for 'dressing' the set, with responsibility for hiring or buying any furnishings or props. It is difficult to get started in film work. However, training in theatre design, or even interior design, may provide a useful starting point followed by possible experience in the theatre or television, before seeking work with a film production company.

Television set design requires a much faster tempo of work. The basic TV design team consists of a designer and design assistant. The designer decides on the shape, size, details and overall design of the set while the assistant carries out working drawings in the

Some specific occupations—a broad guide

form of elevations and ground plans, he also helps the designer dress sets in the studio.

Designers work closely with producers and directors and must have a technical understanding of production processes, together with feeling for the nature of the particular programme. Designers must also translate the producer's intentions and design the scenery and specific camera shots. In addition designers must select and arrange furnishings and properties. A knowledge of the history of art and architecture and everyday things is also important and the ability to draw and convey ideas visually is essential.

Design assistants are usually involved in the preparation of working drawings, ground plans and all the necessary work needed to put the designer's ideas into practical form. The professional background for entry into this work is normally specialised art college training in interior design, exhibition design or theatre design, and training in architectural or exhibition draughtsmanship is normally essential.

3 Textiles/Fashion

Textiles and fashion are separate industries. However although separate they are complementary and inter-related. Certain areas of textile design are influenced by fashion and the fashion-designer, who works with fabrics and materials, must have an understanding of the nature and production of textiles. Although design training is frequently clustered under the joint heading, professional occupations in the trade are quite separtate.

Fashion
Most of the clothing we wear is mass-produced and designed by a designer either working in a large manufacturing company, a small design studio, or as a freelance designer. Dresses, coats, suits, trousers, handbags, millinery, shoes and accessories all make up the world of fashion. Each section influences the other in that accessories, and different garments, all have to come together and relate to each other when we wear an 'outfit'. Fashion and clothing design also includes men's wear and clothes for children and the expanding market of sports and leisure wear.

The field of dress and millinery design is intensely competitive and only the most talented and hard working are likely to succeed. It is very difficult to enter the exclusive world of *haute couture* design but the extension of fashion design into everyday clothes, sports wear and the growth of fashion accessories offer more opportunities for qualified designers. Work in fashion design

Some specific occupations—a broad guide

requires a strong talent and 'flair' combined with a sound basic training. Designers also require practical experience in cutting and making-up, which can be acquired in workrooms and factories.

Most designers have a formal art school training though a few may start on the manufacturing side and develop their design ability by attending art school on a part-time, or evening basis.

(i) Fashion designer

There is great competition for design posts in the fashion industry, especially in the fields of dress design and millinery. Technical knowledge as well as creative ability are required and an awareness of fashion trends is essential, together with technical competence, particularly in pattern cutting.

The dress trade, including coats and suits and millinery, is broadly divided into three sections. These are *haute couture,* wholesale *couture* and wholesale manufacturing.

1 Haute couture

This section of the industry includes the celebrated, well known firms, whose collections of 'model' garments make fashion news each season and tend to establish the trends, in materials, colour and line, which other manufacturers follow.

Haute couture also includes many small, well less known firms, all doing high class work for individual customers. Clothes made for individual customers, or for collections, are largely made by hand—that is why they are so expensive. Each garment may be cut and made individually and much of the intricate sewing may be done by hand.

There are not many openings in this area for the young designer, and in the smaller business *haute couture* firms the designer is often the owner of the business. The designer in this exclusive area of design must always search for highly original ideas and must bear in mind the social habits, tastes and way of life of the people likely to buy his designs. Materials are very important to the designer, who needs a wide knowledge of what is available, and an understanding of how each material may be made up or used. Some leading designers often have materials made specially for them.

Ideas are worked out by drawing and sketching and by draping the material on a stand or model. The dress may first be draped and cut in cheap muslin—the muslin model known as *toile* is then used as a pattern for cutting the actual material. How much of the toile work, cutting of material, and fitting is undertaken by the designer, varies. Usually design assistants, technicians, fitters or

Some specific occupations—a broad guide

cutters, working with the designer in the workroom, carry out this work.

These supporting roles, assisting in the design production, offer some employment opportunities for young designers. In fact it is usually only by getting technical production experience in a fashion workshop, that a young fashion designer can start work.

2 Wholesale couture

Wholesale *couture* houses, or firms, operate in a way which is somewhere between the exclusive *haute couture* companies and the larger wholesale manufacturing companies. Firms in this branch of the fashion trade also make 'model' garments, but the dresses they make are sold to retail shops and not directly to individual customers. Wholesale *couture* firms normally deal with only one shop in an area or town (to maintain the exclusive availability of their garments). They will, however, produce any number of copies of the models for that shop.

Designers working in this field are normally employees of a company and must therefore work within the cost restraints laid down by the directors and follow design and style policy of the company. However, wholesale *couture* designs are original, but the designers usually follow the fashion trends set by the more famous *haute couture* designers.

3 Wholesale manufacturing

The designer in this mass-production branch of the trade works in some ways rather similarly to an individual designer working for any other industry. For example, the fashion designer in a wholesale manufacturing company works as a member of a team, which usually includes the firm's buyer, and production, marketing and costing experts.

The company's buyer selects sample materials from textile manufacturers, and orders materials suitable for the firm's work. The designer produces designs and supervises their cutting and making up by assistants in the workshop. Other members of the design and production team decide how the dresses can be produced in the factory, how long it will take and how much it will cost. The designer therefore works with a team coordinating the work of technicians and assistants, and modifying the design in response to economic and production needs.

The designer in this part of the industry does not work as an original artist to the same degree as a model designer. Wholesale companies usually make thousands of garments in one style and must therefore ensure that the style will be popular with the

Some specific occupations — a broad guide

buying public. Wholesale firms generally tend to adapt and follow the fashions set by the model houses, it is a design process of selection and adaption, bearing in mind very much popular taste, market trends and costs.

Designers working in wholesale manufacturing are usually sent to see the 'collections' and sometimes even buy patterns, toiles or designs from the *haute couture* houses. In addition to seeing collections designers must be constantly aware of what is going on internationally and keep up to date with all the major trends. When a design is agreed the designer normally makes working drawings for cutting a sample garment, which is used in explaining to technicians, and sample hands, how the dress is to be made up.

Wholesale manufacturing companies usually employ staff designers and workshop assistants but also commission drawings from freelance designers. Job opportunities are more frequently found in the wholesale trade, particularly as design assistants, pattern cutters or toile artists.

(ii) Millinery

Millinery design and production, or more simply hats and headresses, follows exactly the industrial structure of the fashion designer. In other words the millinery trade has *haute couture,* wholesale *couture* and wholesale manufacturing sections.

As with dressware it is the model house who generally set the trends and fashions. These are first adapted by the wholesale model houses (or wholesale *couture* firms) and then the designs are picked up by the large manufacturers who produce hats by mass-production. Some milliners are trained at college while others may learn the craft in small workshops and graduate to designing by attending college on a release basis. As with dress design the smaller *couture* firms are usually owned by the designer, who has set up his own small workshop to both design and produce hats, usually for an exclusive range of individual customers.

(iii) Shoes

The shoe industry, like many forms of mass-production has two main branches. The mass-produced industry for the cheaper range of shoes and small workshops producing limited numbers of exclusive designs. While the larger manufacturers tend to produce for the high street shops, the small craft workshops either produce specially for individual clients, or fashion houses, or for exclusive retail outlets.

Designers for the shoe industry may therefore work as staff designers for large manufacturers, or on a freelance basis for small

Some specific occupations—a broad guide

workshops or large companies. Some particularly talented designers have their own small workshops, producing designs for a specialist market.

Staff designers prepare a new season's range in conjunction with production and sales department staff. Master patterns, of the shapes of the different shoe parts, have to be produced from drawings or models submitted by the designer. Working patterns for production are then made from the master patterns. In many of the smaller firms the designer works as a pattern cutter, though larger firms usually employ both specialist designers and separate pattern cutters. Shoe designers must however have a good working knowledge of production methods, materials and pattern cutting.

(iv) Embroidery
Many of our clothes and accessories are embroidered and industrial embroidery is part of the fashion industry. Embroidery is either produced by hand or machine. Hand embroidery obviously demands considerable skill and is used on more expensive garments and items. Firms producing embroidery are mainly small units and they employ more skilled operators and craftspeople than designers. In other words there are more openings for craftwork than for actually designing.

Some fashion designers, particularly in the *haute couture* section, either produce their own designs for embroidery or commission freelance designers. In general, however, this is a branch of the industry which tends to use few designers but many craftworkers.

In addition to industrial embroidery, related to the fashion and clothing industry, there is a completely separate market for the artist-designer embroiderer. Such work is not, in any way, associated with industrial activity, with craftspeople producing decorative embroidery and wall hangings, usually for the retail craft market and occasional commercial or ecclesiastical commissions. Training for this craft is normally part of constructed textile design courses.

(v) Lingerie and corsetry
Designing lingerie requires a sound knowledge of fashion trends and styles. Lingerie reflects what is happening in dress design and the design of undergarments must change and respond to the styles and shapes being used in fashion design. The wide range of fabrics and man-made fibres available to the industry has in recent years revolutionised the openings for designers. Like all branches of the fashion industry the lingerie trade has small firms making exclusive models for individual customers, and other small firms

Some specific occupations—a broad guide

producing limited quantities of expensive garments for sale to selected shops, and larger manufacturers mass-producing a wide range of styles for the high street trade.

Some fashion designers also design lingerie and it is therefore not entirely a specialist design field. Corsetry however is a distinct and special branch of the clothing industry. Designers of corsetry must have some knowledge of human anatomy, and how and where support should be given. Designers must be aware of the shapes required by fashion, as even the human shape can vary at the demand of fashion, and they must also know how to correct aspects of the figure and posture. Trade training, combined with college study, are usually necessary for this type of work which is a specialist field of dress design.

(vi) Fashion accessories
The world of fashion accessories is a strange mixture in terms of the ways in which goods are produced and designed. Accessories include such things as belts, buckles, buttons, handbags, gloves, all of which are made and designed in a variety of ways. Fashion accessories offer opportunities for designers working for industry, freelance designers and craftsmen-designers, who design and make.

For the mass-produced, cheaper market, large firms may employ staff designers or more frequently commission occasional freelance designs. Small workshops and firms usually work to order from fashion houses or for particular commissions and retail outlets. Craftsmen-designers in fashion accessories work in two ways. Having set up their own workshop the craftsman either designs and makes up limited ranges for special orders, sometimes from fashion houses, or produces accessories, whatever these are, and finds his or her own retail outlet, like any other craftsman working in this way.

(vii) Menswear—sportswear
Although the majority of work in the fashion industry is related to women's wear it will be very wrong to imagine that all design work was focused on this work. In recent years there has been an enormous development in the design of men's wear, leisure clothes and sports wear. New fabrics and interesting combinations of fabrics, and new effects of cutting, have created new opportunities for the designer. Designers in this field must have complete knowledge of cutting, tailoring and manufacturing processes. But with this technical background and creative ability, combined particularly with the explosion in leisure wear goods, openings for designers are increasing in this field.

Some specific occupations—a broad guide

(viii) Associated occupations

The fashion designer is supported by a whole range of technical experts and the fashion industry also provides a number of other associated specialist occupations. These include the following:

Technicians

All fashion designers, and fashion workshops, require the technical skills of pattern cutters, fitters, making-up specialists, or sample hands. Knowledge of the technical processes needed to translate an idea on paper, or a toile model, into production are essential to the designer. The designer cannot however do all these things and specialist technicians are trained by fashion schools to do this. A fashion technician may cover several processes, or specialise in one area, such as pattern cutting. Technicians usually work closely with designers and sometimes learn their skills in the trade with possibly some release for college training.

Fashion illustrator

Fashion drawing is sometimes used to illustrate fashion magazines and for catalogues or advertisements. Wholesale dress houses regularly require fashion illustrators for their catalogues. Some fashion houses employ their own fashion illustrators, while others may work in graphic design studios, and specialise in this work—other illustrators work on a freelance basis. Many fashion illustrators may have trained originally as a fashion designer, and developed a special skill for this type of work, and all fashion illustrators certainly need a thorough knowledge of fashion as well as skill as an illustrator.

Fashion journalism

The fashion industry produces a large number of magazines and journals—in fact the trade is dependent on these periodicals, not not only for conveying ideas and trends between fashion houses and retail outlets, but also in interesting the buying public in the latest clothes and styles. Fashion journalism is therefore a specialist field where the writers must have a thorough technical knowledge of dress making and production, and of the fashion industry and retail market.

Some training courses in fashion journalism are available but many journalists in this field were initially trained as fashion designers, which can provide a good basis for this work. Journalists are either employed by one magazine, on the editorial staff, or work as freelance writers for a number of periodicals.

Some specific occupations—a broad guide
Fashion buyer
Large stores and groups of shops employ fashion buyers responsible for the purchasing policy of the shop or company. Buyers must have a very thorough knowledge of the fashion industry and be familiar with all the current fashion trends and likely innovations and changes. In addition buyers must know what is likely to sell. This requires a knowledge of what the public wants and the nature of the particular market served by the company the buyer works for. Being able to judge what will sell, and what the public may want, or be persuaded to want, is a considerable skill and the wholesale manufacturing branch of the fashion industry depends on the skill of the buyer to a large extent.

Buyers are therefore normally senior appointments and usually have had previous experience either in the fashion trade or retail industry.

Paper pattern design
Home dressmaking is a large industry and a few designers are employed by firms who make paper patterns, for dresses, lingerie and children's garments, and some men's wear. The patterns usually follow existing styles and must be simple enough to be made up successfully by amateur home dressmakers; though sometimes they may be used by professional retail dressmakers.

Some pattern making firms buy models from famous designers and cut patterns from these which are often called *'couturier'* patterns and are more expensive than normal patterns. Paper pattern makers work in the same way as in the wholesale dress trade, except that no actual dress materials are used. Designers or technicians who are experienced pattern cutters in the trade may therefore sometimes become pattern designers.

(ix) Theatrical costume design
Theatrical costume designers work in a number of ways and are employed by a variety of organisations. Designers may work for film companies or theatrical costumers, a large theatre company or, most frequently, for the television companies and the BBC. The BBC, for example, has a large costume department and employs full-time costume designers and costume assistants. Designers in this field should have a sound training in design (fashion design or theatre design) with a knowledge and interest in the history of fashion. Costume designers also need to have a wide knowledge of materials, the qualities, costs, how they will drape and, if working in film or television, how they will photograph. A thorough knowledge of dress making and pattern cutting is also needed (hence the advantage of a fashion training). Costume

Some specific occupations—a broad guide

designers work either as full-time designers with a firm of theatrical costumers, or a television company, or may be under contract to a theatrical or film company. Designers may also work on a freelance basis, but need experience of production workshops before working in this way. Many designers therefore gain technical and production experience first, as a costume assistant, and then possibly move into freelance design work.

Whereas a costume designer is responsible for devising and designing costumes, and requires a design training, a costume assistant is required to help select and fit suitable costumes and liaise with suppliers, costumiers and the work room, and sometimes represent the designer at rehersals or filming sessions. Though it is not always necessary for an assistant to have a professional design training it would normally not be possible to gain promotion to a costume designer without such college training.

Textiles design

Textiles design, as we have seen in chapter three, is a rather misleading title for what in fact is an industry covering a wide variety of work. The term textiles in fact covers all manner of materials from woven and printed fabrics to furnishing fabrics, carpets, curtains, wallpapers, floorcoverings and the whole range of decorated surfaces including vinyl and printed plastics. Textile designers normally specialise in one area but freelance designers may frequently design for different branches of the textiles or 'surface decoration' industry.

(x) Woven fabrics

The weaving industry, in simple terms, has two very distinct elements; the highly technical industrial production and the small designer-craftsman workshop.

To work in industry the designer must have a thorough knowledge of textile technology and production processes. Fabrics are not always made of one material and may for example be mixtures of wool, cotton, flax, rayon, silk, nylon and other man-made fibres. The designer must understand the qualities of the various yarns and know how each will influence the appearance, texture, durability and cost of the fabric. The design of woven fabrics is also determined, to a large extent, by the limitations of the machines used.

Training in machine technology may be obtained in colleges of technology or by design apprenticeships, as well as in art schools, but obtaining the necessary technical experience is essential. In fact fabric production is a high technology industry and designers

Some specific occupations—a broad guide

must have experience of this. There is also considerable specialisation in the fabric industry and designers are seldom expert in more than one type of fabric.

Designs are produced in a number of ways usually beginning with a drawing which is set out as a specification and passed to technicians, who weave a sample length. From this sample, adjustments are made until it is ready and acceptable for production. Designers are sometimes responsible for both the pattern and the cloth, though when a pattern is woven into a material, such as a brocade or damask, then two designers may work together, one on the material and the other on the pattern.

For some forms of production, such as furnishing fabrics, an art school training and hand-loom experience is preferred, while other work requires more knowledge of factory production and textile technology. Much design for woven fabrics is carried out by staff designers in factory studios, so that the maximum cooperation between the designer and technical staff may be achieved. Freelance work is sometimes accepted, but usually only if the designer has sufficient technical and production experience.

There are, in the textiles industry, opportunities for work as *design managers*. Students who have studied design management as part of their training in textile technology can help bridge the gap between creative designer and technical production. A design manager is primarily a technologist with an understanding of design, and it is he or she who can commission freelance designers and translate, as it were, their ideas into production reality.

In addition to the mass-production fabric industry there are also outlets and opportunities for hand-loom design and production. Craftsman-designers in weaving, often set up their own workshops, studios, or small businesses and produce fabrics for direct sale to retail outlets or individual customers. Hand production is rather slow, so artist designed and produced fabrics are more expensive, but there is certainly a market for such quality production. Craft hand weavers may of course obtain additional work as occasional freelance designers for industry. Some studios are also run as small businesses and combine hand-loom work with power production and may therefore supply larger stores and retail outlets.

(xi) Knitwear

Closely associated to the woven fabric industry is the knitwear trade. In recent years knitwear has come very much back into fashion and, with the ready availability of new knitting machines, flourishing small craft based industries and workshops have developed.

Some specific occupations—a broad guide

The designer-craftsman in knitting can, with the purchase of small industrial knitting machines, both design and produce knitwear for retail outlets, including for example small fashion boutiques and craft shops. The revival of this craft industry has given employment to many designers and craftsmen, and is frequently associated with weaving. For example, many small workshops, set up by designers, may combine both weaving and knitwear.

The knitwear industry, producing garments for the mass market, also employs designers. Much work is however based on traditional patterns and designs, so work for designers in certain firms is rather limited. New designs and patterns are however being introduced in some areas, usually where designers are either employed as a staff designer, or where freelance designs are commissioned.

(xii) Lace

There are very many uses for lace work which can basically be divided into furnishing laces—curtains, bedspreads, tablecloths and dress laces—blouses, lingerie, dresses, trimmings. Dress lace is really an accessory of the fashion trade and designers in this area must understand the nature of fashion and its changing trends. Lace is made from a variety of materials including silk, cotton, rayon, nylon and manufacturers usually specialise in one type of lace work as the machinery is complicated and expensive.

People buy lace very much because of its visual appeal. Lace has no real utilitarian purpose—it does not keep you warm or cover you up. The visual design or pattern work is therefore vitally important. Many designs are of course traditional, but there is scope for new designs in this field. Largely because of the complicated nature of the machines (as in the weaving industry), the process of lace designing is divided between the designer and a draughtsperson. The designer is primarily concerned with drawing or creating the patterns, though he must have some knowledge of how the machinery works, while the draughtsperson translates these drawings onto squared paper, setting them out ready for machine production. The draughtsperson therefore has to have a very thorough knowledge and understanding of the machinery and how it works, and combines a sensitivity for the artists' designs and the limitations and scope of the production technology. Some designers may draw out their own designs, but this is rather rare. Designers and draughtspeople may come from art school, or may learn their skills while working with a manufacturer. Training for draughtsmen is only available in lace making areas of the country, though the designer may not have specialised in design for lace but

Some specific occupations—a broad guide

may have studied textile design on a broader basis.

(xiii) Printed textiles
Unlike woven fabrics and lace work the designer for printed textiles does not need to know a great deal about production processes, in that printing processes onto fabrics are much simpler than actually constructing the fabric itself. The designer must of course have a working knowledge of different printing processes but the gap between the technology of production and the designer is not as large as in some branches of the industry.

Printed textile design is an overcrowded field and it is difficult sometimes for freelance designers to initially get work without very real ability. A high level of draughtsmanship is required and generally the designer does not work in the factory where the textiles are printed but usually in a commercial studio from where manufacturers buy designs. Commercial studios employ beginners, both from secondary schools and art schools. Art school leavers cannot, to start with, expect to undertake much creative work, they are much more likely to find themselves doing routine draughtsmanship tasks, such as working out repeat patterns, or re-colouring someone else's design.

Some manufacturers employ staff designers, as well as buying designs from studios, but the staff designer's job may include adapting and re-colouring purchased designs as well as creating some original designs. More frequently manufacturers may employ design managers or manageresses whose job is to organise the flow of printed designs from original art work to finished product. This will involve contact with customers, freelance designers, print factories and commercial design studios—in fact the design manager is the person who normally buys the designs from the studios.

Commercial studio work is frequently rather routine and repetitive and designers therefore frequently try to move into consultancy work, where they may be retained by a number of manufacturers to advise on designs and submit new designs themselves—or to work as freelance designers trying to sell their designs direct to manufacturers.

(xiv) Wall paper design
Wall paper designers work in very much the same way as textile designers except that their designs are normally printed on paper rather than fabric. In fact some commercial studios produce designs for both wall paper and textiles manufacturers and freelance designers in this field frequently also design textiles. The wall paper industry in recent years has expanded to include a wide

Some specific occupations—a broad guide

variety of wall coverings, not only wall papers, and opportunities for the design of vinyls and wall tiles have, for example, extended the scope for designers. The majority of design work for the wall covering industry is purchased from commercial studios but the larger manufacturing companies are likely to employ a design manager, and staff designers, along with assistants who are sometimes known as 'colourists'. A colourist's work is normally to hand colour original schemes and prepare art work for printing.

(xv) Carpets
As with woven textiles, carpet designers must have a working knowledge of the looms used to produce carpets. It is a complex production process and the designer once again has to work closely with the technical production team. With the growth of interest in interior design, and developments in home decoration, there is now certainly more scope for the carpet designer. Historically, and until fairly recently, the carpet industry tended to use only traditional designs, which were produced with little adaption and without needing the skills of a designer. However, there is now a growing demand for original carpet designs, not just for private use, but for hotels, large offices, liners and hotels. Carpets designed for such large users are usually contract work. This means that a carpet designer is commissioned or 'contracted' to produce designs for a specific interior. Frequently this type of contract work is very rewarding as it gives the designer the opportunity to possibly work with the interior designer or architect, and design the carpet to relate to the other furnishings and the shape, size and function of the room or building.

The designer sets his pattern out in colour on squared paper, each square representing one tuft of wool in the carpet. The whole carpet is not usually set out like this, only a section which can be repeated. Copyists are employed to help draw out the pattern and colour alternative schemes. Copyist and colourists can have an art school training and may work up to be designers through this work, though some assistants learn their crafts in the factory workshop and drawing office. Usually after art school the young designer does in fact start work as a copyist, gaining further experience in the factory.

Freelance or consultant carpet designers, often work in association with interior designers and a knowledge of interior design is certainly helpful to the designer of carpets.

(xvi.) Plastics, decorative surfaces, floor coverings
Extensive developments in recent years of all manner of plastic, vinyl and melamine surfaces has not only revolutionised interior

Some specific occupations—a broad guide

decoration but provided further outlets for textile designers. Hard, heat resistant and washable plastic sheeting and tiles have altered the look of our kitchens, bathrooms, restaurants and interiors. All these surfaces have to be designed, and many 'textile' designers see themselves now more as designers of decorative surfaces, whatever material they are made in.

Some specialist firms in this field employ full-time design staff while other companies buy designs from commercial studios or commission work on a freelance basis.

4 Fine Art

We clearly live in a world where no regular occupations can unfortunately be listed for painters, sculptors, and printmakers. We have already discussed how fine artists may find work in all manner of related occupations and how 'fine art' as a subject does not set out to necessarily provide a vocational training, but rather a broader personal form of education.

However, in addition to all the many diverse outlets artists may find for their work and ideas, a number of specific jobs may be seen to relate to a fine art training.

(i) Art and design historian

Some fine artists may, as part of their training, become interested in art history and take up further study in this subject. Art historians work predominantly in education as teachers, mainly in colleges of art and universities, but opportunities also exist for work in museums and art galleries where art historians may work as curators, archivists, education officers, cataloguers or museum assistants.

As the role of the art historian broadens, to include design history, some jobs may be found in the field of industrial design archive work where large companies, with distinguished traditions, require historians to maintain or research their historic records and, in some cases, company collections or museums. Art historians may also become involved in arts criticism—that is writing and commentating on design and the arts—and some art and design historians may therefore undertake freelance work reviewing exhibitions, working as art critics or writing books on their area of specialist research.

Art and picture dealers also employ, and need to consult with, art historians from time to time and some large companies, including for example Christies and Sothebys (the famous London based international dealers) offer courses of training. These courses, lasting from several months to a year, cover the history of fine and decorative arts and include work on cataloguing and

Some specific occupations—a broad guide

valuing works of art, and study of the art market. The fees for these courses are however high, and no grants are available.

(ii) Museum and gallery curatorship—exhibition and museum assistants
Work in galleries and museums is varied and usually requires qualifications in librarianship, art history and curatorship (such as the Museums Association's Diploma). A fine art background may be acceptable particularly if it combines a further qualification in, for example, art history or librarianship.

Gallery and museum work includes all manner of activities ranging from administrative duties to preparing catalogues, packing exhibitions for touring, hanging exhibitions, historical and education work, conservation and research. In large galleries and museums this work is carried out by separate specialists but in small galleries this has to be combined, with individual staff undertaking a wide range of activities. As in most occupations senior posts clearly go to well qualified and experienced candidates. Galleries and museums normally appoint assistant staff usually to undertake the broader range of more general duties, including indexing and listing exhibits, minor conservation, storage and transportation of exhibits, with some cataloguing and administrative duties.

Professional qualifications in librarianship, curatorship or art history are the normal routes but artists and sculptors, with a strong interest in this field, may find suitable openings.

The design of exhibitions, the display of exhibits, and the communication of visual information to the public, is normally the work of specialists in exhibition design, display or graphics and is not normally part of museum curatorship.

(iii) Picture restoration—preservation, conservation—the paper conservator
Some courses in fine art include work in picture restoration and a few major art galleries, picture dealers and museums offer limited training opportunities in picture restoration and preservation. (See addresses on page 152, and publications on page 146).

Picture restoration can of course be associated, not only with large public galleries and museums, but with smaller private commercial galleries and the antique trade. Full-time posts in picture restoration are normally found in large galleries and museums but individual freelance work, particularly in connection with the antique trade and small galleries, offers career opportunities for those skilled and trained in this area. Picture restoration takes many forms as paintings are made on many

Some specific occupations — a broad guide

different materials, such as paper, canvas, board or, in the case of murals, walls.

Work concerned with the conservation or restoration of drawings or water colour paintings on paper, is usually the job of the *Paper Conservator*. Paper conservation is a specialised occupation with specific professional training (Camberwell School of Art offers a course, and see also the Museums Association page 155).

Most of the material in our galleries and museums is of course on paper, and paper conservation therefore involves treating manuscripts, books, documents, photographs, drawings, paintings, charts and maps.

The paper conservator's work is usually associated with large libraries, museums, galleries and private collections and frequently is combined with a skill or knowledge of *Bookbinding* (see page 108). The conservator's work combines a high level of craft skill, considerable technical knowledge, and ideally an understanding of painting, drawings and designed objects.

Conservation work is also necessary in all other craft and design fields and craftsmen and designers, with knowledge of a specific area, may often find employment in restoring work for museums, dealers or galleries. Large public museums and galleries and art dealers normally have departments of conservation and with the growing interest in our historic and cultural traditions the role of the conservator is an important occupation in art and design.

(iv) Picture research — picture and slide librarian

Libraries, advertising agencies, film and television companies and some publishers require the services of picture researchers. Work in this area normally requires a first degree, some knowledge of librarianship and a strong visual sense and awareness (a graduate in fine art would usually need further training in aspects of librarianship).

Books are now no longer the only form in which knowledge is stored and the growth of visual collections, slide libraries, and audio visual material, has began to provide openings for people with visual knowledge. A picture researcher may need a knowledge of photography and information storage systems, and will either collect pictorial material or be concerned with its documentation and cataloguing.

(v) The community arts — arts administration

In recent years there have been significant developments in trying to bring the arts into more everyday contact with the community. Most towns, counties, major boroughs or regions have set up arts centres, associations or services aimed to help the arts benefit the

Some specific occupations—a broad guide

community as a whole.

The majority of jobs in the local authority and community arts service require a combination of administrative and creative skills. Arts centres normally offer a wide variety of activities, in all the arts, including painting, sculpture, film, literature, music, and drama; and the work of arts officers usually includes elements of creative practice, organisation, management and administrative skills. Practising artists may often find rewarding work in the local arts service but ability as an artist has sometimes to be supplemented with training in other fields, such as administration or education.

In addition to full-time posts, administrating or organising the work of the arts centres, jobs also exist for part-time or limited tenure work as artists in residence at art centres or on specific community arts projects. Such work may either include helping local people with a particular project, or teaching at a centre on a part-time basis, or even working at the centre as an artist; giving local people a chance to meet an 'artist at work'.

In addition to the work of local arts and community centres some authorities employ advisers or organisers responsible for developing, administering and encouraging the arts within a town, region or area. Students on fine art would normally require working experience in community centres, or a further qualification, in for example arts administration or possibly education, before applying for such work. General or combined degrees in the Arts, or inter-disciplinary courses, where art and social science, education or history have been studied are useful qualifcations for work in this field. Senior appointments as, for example, an Arts Centre Director or Adviser would require working experience in the community arts, an informed interest in all the arts, with ideally some practical experience, and a diploma in Arts Administration.

(vi) Work as a painter, or printmaker—a summary
In reality, as we have already seen, there are no defined occupations for the painter or sculptor. Painters and artists normally have to find other work which hopefully provides them with sufficient free time to continue developing their own work and ideas.

Part-time teaching in schools or colleges, formally helped many artist, but opportunities for teaching have recently been drastically reduced by cuts in public expenditure. We have already dealt with how artists may work on their own and take every opportunity to exhibit their work and bring it to the public's notice, but it would be misleading to assume that no outlets whatsoever exist for

Some specific occupations—a broad guide

paintings, prints and sculpture. Artists do continue producing painting, and works of art, and we see these in our galleries, museums, public buildings, offices, factories and homes. There is therefore work for artists—and a market for their work if they are talented and gifted. The demand however is such that most artists, however able, need some form of other regular income to support them while waiting for commissions, exhibitions or work to be sold. In addition to other supporting work artists often find an outlet for their talents in associated fields such as the cinema, advertising, television, the theatre, popular music and the media—all areas where creative imagination, flair and talent are needed. Artists, as we have seen, must be imaginative and resourceful people and should therefore, by the nature of their training, be versatile in looking for outlets for their personal ideas and creative imaginations.

In addition to finding employment in teaching, or some of the associated occupations already referred to, some work for *artists in residence* is occasionally advertised. Arts centres, colleges, polytechnics, universities and even museums, from time to time, offer opportunities for artists to work in this way. This work is always only for a limited period but can help, particularly the young artist, trying to establish a reputation or preparing work for an exhibition.

5 Art and design teaching

In chapter three the basic routes towards training as an art teacher were outlined in some detail (see page 64) and the broad differences between work in primary, secondary and higher education discussed. These are however briefly re-stated here along with some other possible areas of work in art education. It should be remembered that teaching is not in any way restricted to schools and that there are an increasing number of opportunities in other institutions, where art education is needed.

Opportunities for work in art teaching, both full-time and part-time have recently been severely reduced. Cuts in public spending and a fall in the school population, due to changing birth rate patterns, have unfortunately reduced the number of teaching posts available.

(i) Primary teaching

Art is not normally taught as a specialist subject with this age group but creative work, in all manner of materials, is seen as a major vehicle for learning with young children. Opportunities for a lot of painting, modelling and creative work should therefore be given to young children though teachers of this age group are normally not art specialists; but qualified teachers, with some interest in art, or who have taken art as a main subject while at college.

(ii) Secondary schools
Art and design in secondary schools is normally taught as a specialist subject by a qualified teacher who has either attended art college, and then taken a one-year post-graduate education course, or obtained a degree in education with art and design as a main subject.

There is at present a nationwide drive to improve the level of design understanding and design education. Teachers of design are not only those working in the craft and technology areas but also the art teacher, who should normally play a leading role in developing strong visual awareness and a critical sense, and understanding, of all the designed objects around us. Many designers, industrialists, educationalists, (and even some politicians) recognise that the future of the country, in terms of its manufacturing success, and quality of urban life, rest very much on the quality of design education in schools. So there is particularly valuable work to be done by trained design teachers in this field.

(iii) Further and higher education
Normally art and design in further and higher education is taught as a highly specialised subject, training designers for a particular profession. Teachers therefore in colleges, or departments of art and design, are normally appointed on a basis of their professional experience and skill. A teaching qualification is not necessary for higher education in art and design but what is essential is a high level of distinguished professional practice, and experience in a given field. A large majority of teachers in art colleges are employed on a part-time basis so that the designer may continue with his or her professional practice. This is a very important aspect of design training as it forms a natural link between the world of the student in college and industrial reality.

Although most part-time staff are highly experienced professionals, some appointments are given to young talented designers just starting their careers. This has the advantage of bringing fresh bright ideas into the college and also gives the young designer some help and support, while he or she is trying to establish themselves in the industrial world. Unfortunately, recent cuts in expenditure for higher education has drastically reduced the number of openings for part-time teaching.

In additon to specialist art and design training in higher

Some specific occupations—a broad guide

education some colleges of further education provide art, or art history as a liberal or complementary study, or as an 'A' level subject. The teaching in these departments is normally undertaken by qualified specialist art teachers and art historians, usually with some previous teaching experience, rather than practising designers or artists with industrial experience.

(iv) Art teaching in other institutions

There are numerous other opportunities for art teachers outside formal teaching in schools and colleges. Art education has a broad social and human context and its value is seen in many other institutions. We have already referred (in the section on opportunities in Fine Art—see page 135) to the work of the artist in **Museums and Galleries,** as education officers or members of the gallery's education staff. Most galleries and museums have education departments, sometimes associated with the local authority, and these offer opportunities to qualified art teachers, usually with some previous teaching experience, and an interest in art history or museum studies.

Local arts centres also employ art teachers and **community arts projects** frequently need the help of qualified teachers. Many art centres are operated by local education authorities who employ teachers, sometimes on a part-time basis, to work in this branch of education.

Arts administration officers are also often qualified teachers as part of their work involves bringing the arts into the local schools.

The education authorities of most cities and towns also provide a wide range of **recreational evening classes** in art and crafts. This type of evening institute work provides opportunities for part-time teaching, and many artists find this not only rewarding, but helpful in giving them time in the day to continue their own work as painters or craftsmen.

Art and crafts also play an important part in the work of the **prison service.** Teachers of art and craft may find part-time work teaching in HM Prisons and Borstals. This is obviously a very special branch of art education, calling for particular skills and understanding, which is seen as a way of helping people in terms of personal therapy, rehabilitation and self expression.

Art therapy also uses art and craft activities to help people. This is a small but growing profession with art therapists working in general hospitals, psychiatric units, and helping the aged and physically and mentally handicapped in hospitals, day centres and schools.

Art therapists work alongside psychiatrists and psychotherapists and, as well as being a teacher, they need also to have an

Some specific occupations—a broad guide

understanding of psychopathology, which is studied as part of therapy training. Most entrants to art therapy are graduates, usually in art and design subjects or sometimes in education, psychology or sociology, where this is combined with a real ability in art. Some hospitals and schools occasionally employ practising artists on a part-time basis to help in this work. There are courses of professional training to qualify you as an art therapist which may be entered by graduates, usually after some relevant experience. Contact the British Association of Art Therapists for details, see page 152.

Notes on Bibliography and Addresses
1 Journals and periodicals
Reading periodicals or journals related to your particular field of interest is an important part of developing professional knowledge and awareness. The periodicals listed carry advertisements for employment and other opportunities.

The Arts Council issues monthly vacancy lists (on receipt of a stamped addressed envelope), though these are mainly taken from newspapers and magazines.

The national press also advertise jobs, particularly the *Guardian* (Monday—creative and media), *Daily Telegraph, Times* and *Observer. The Listener, New Society, Times Educational Supplement, The Stage, Time Out, Tribune* and *City Limits* are among other useful sources for information and job vacancies.

2 Bibliography
The majority of the titles, included in this section, are available from school, public or career service libraries. Many of the smaller publications are distributed free but a stamped addressed envelope is generally required. For addresses see pages 148-49.

3 Addresses
The addresses included in no way form a definitive list, but space has limited the choice to those most closely related to careers and professions. The addresses of Faculties, Colleges and Schools of Art and Design may easily be obtained from many sources and publications, and have therefore not been included. The telephone directory will have the address of your local College and full national lists are included in the Design Council publication 'Design Courses in Britain', 'The Arts Review Year Book' or the 'The Educaton Authorities Directory and Annual' available for reference at school and public libraries. Full regional information and course lists are available from Regional Advisory Council.

Bibliography and Addresses

1 Journals and Periodicals
carrying job advertisements and information

General – Art and Design
Arts Monthly
Arts Newsletter – 17 Shakespeare Terrace, Sunderland, Tyne and Wear SR2 7JG
Arts Review
Art Services Newsletter – 6-8 Rosebery Avenue, London EC1
Crafts – Crafts Council magazine
Design – Design Council magazine
Designer – Journal of the Society of Industrial Artists and Designers
Crafts Quarterly – 17 Shakespeare Terrace, Sunderland, Tyne and Wear SR2 7JG

Specific Subjects
Advertisers' Weekly
Amateur Photographer
Apollo
British Clothing Manufacturer – Textile Trade Publication 23-49 Emerald Street, London WC1
British Journal of Photography
Campaign – advertising, graphic design, publishing, etc
Ceramics Review
Clothing and Footwear Journal
Community Care – art therapy, community arts, etc
Drapers' Record
Fashion Weekly
Federation of British Craft Societies Newsletter – 43 Earlham Street, London WC2H 9LD
Illustration – magazine of Association of Illustrators
Inscape – journal of the British Association of Art Therapists
Interior Design
Knitting International
Manufacturing Clothier
Museums Bulletin – journal of the Museums Association
Opportunities – museums, arts administration, community arts, available in public libraries
Sight and Sound

2 Bibliography
General art and design career books, pamphlets and leaflets

After 'A' Level—published by the National Foundation for Educational Research

A Career in Art and Design—free leaflet issued by the Technician Education Council

Careers in Design—free leaflet issued by the Design Council

Careers in Art and Design—by Linda Ball, Kogan Page 1980

CNAA Directory of First Degree and Diploma of Education Courses—annual publication from CNAA

A Compendium of Advanced Courses in Colleges of Further and Higher Education—published on behalf of Regional Advisory Council by the London and Home Counties Regional Advisory Council for Technological Education

CRAC Degree Course Guides, Art and Design (including Art History)—available from, Careers Research and Advisory Centre (CRAC)

Design Courses in Britain 1982-83—Design Council publication

Degree Course Guides (Art and Design—published CRAC/Hobson Press

Directory of Further Education—CRAC/Hobson Press publication

Graduate Studies—CRAC/Hobson Press publication

A Guide for Applicants to Universities, Polytechnics and other colleges offering degrees—by Peter David, Advisory Centre for Education, 18 Victoria Park Square, London E2 9BP

Handbook of Degree and Advanced Courses in Institutes/Colleges of Higher Education, Polytechnics, University Departments of Education—published by Lund Humphries, annually

On From 'A' Levels, Choose Your Course—free booklet from Department of Education and Science

Other Careers: Earning a Living in the Arts and Media—published Wildwood House 1973

Polytechnic Handbook—published Lund Humphries, annually

Signposts—a boxed set of career information cards. Available from Careers and Occupational Information Centre (COIC)

Signposts to Higher Education—available free of charge from the Department of Education and Science

Signposts for Sixth Formers—by Edwin H Cox, Careers Consultants Limited

The Professional Practice of Design—by Dorothy Goslett, Batsford

Time Between—published by CRAC

UCCA Handbook—issued by the Universities Central Council on Admissions

Bibliography
Information Leaflet 1982-83 — issued free by UCCA
Which Degree — published annually by Haymarket Publishing
Your Choice at 17 + — published by CRAC

Student grants
Directory of Grant Making Trusts — edited W S. Mooney, Charities Aid Foundation
Education Charities — published by National Union of Students
Grants to Students, Pamphlets No 1 and 2 — available from the Department of Education and Science
Grants Handbook — Published by National Union of Students
The Grants Register — published by Macmillan
Guide to Students' Allowances — available, free of charge from the Scottish Education Department Awards Branch, Haymarket House, Clifton Terrace, Edinburgh
Industrial Awards and the universities central admission scheme — issued free of charge by UCCA
Sponsorships to students following first degrees, BEC and TEC higher awards, or comparable courses beginning in 1982 — published by Careers and Occupational Information Centre Manpower Services Commission, Moorfoot, Sheffield S1 4PQ

Advice on setting up workshops and self employment
Artlaw, collected articles from ART MONTHLY — available from Artlaw Services, 358 Strand, London WC2
CoSIRA publications — *available from The Council for Small Industries in Rural Areas*
  Craft Workshops in the English Countryside
  List of Organisers in England and Wales
  Financing Expansion in Small Rural Areas
  Services to Small Rural Business
  Increase Profitability
Crafts Council Publications
  Setting up a Workshop — edited by John Crowe
  Grants and Loans
  Setting Up Scheme
  Workshop Assistant Scheme
  Advanced Training Scheme
  Bursaries — Conditions
  Grants and Loans Schemes
Creating Your Own Work — by Micheline Mason, Gresham Books, 1980
Earning Money at Home — by Edith Rudinger, Consumers' Association 1979

Bibliography

The Guardian Guide to Running a Small Business—by Clive Woodstock, Kogan Page
Guide to Awards and Schemes—published annually by the Arts Council of Great Britain
How to Establish Your Own Studio—information leaflet available from Arts Services Grants and Space (SPACE)
How to Start and Run Your Own Business—by M Mogana, Graham and Trotman Ltd 1980
Minding Your Own Business—how to set up a small business. Published by (COIC)
Occupation Self Employed—by Rosemary Peltit, Wildwood House 1977
Small Firms Information Service—free leaflets available from the Small Firms Information Service, Department of Industry
Small Business Kit—available from the National Extension College, 18 Booklands Avenue, Cambridge CB2 2HN
Sources of Finance and Advice for Artists and Craftsmen—by Ginny Winstone, available from the University of Sussex
Starting in Business (IR 28)—free leaflet, available from the Inland Revenue
Work for Yourself—by Chris Parsons and Angela Neustatter, Pan Books Ltd 1980
Working for Yourself, a Daily Telegraph Guide—by Godfrey Golzen, Kogan Page

Specific subjects

Art history

Careers for History of Art Graduates—available from Aberdeen University Careers and Appointments Service, Humanity Manse, College Bounds, Old Aberdeen AB9 2UX

Conservation/Restoration

Conservation in Museums and Galleries—International Institute for Conservation of Historic and Artistic Works (UK Group) 1974
Conservation Sourcebook—published Crafts Council 1979
Crafts Council Conservation Section—free leaflet from Crafts Council

Fashion/Textiles

ABC of Fashion and Design—Dunn, published Failsham 1973
Fashion Director—What She Does and How To Be One—Jabenis (Wiley) 1972

Bibliography
Fashion Marketing — published Allen and Unwin 1973
Fashion Merchandising — by Traxelle and Juddle, published McGraw 1975
Inside the Fashion Business — by Janow and Juddle, published Wiley 1974
Opportunities for Graduates in Textile Design — Manchester University Careers Service 1979
Post 'A' Level Education and Training for the Clothing Industry — published by the Clothing and Allied Products Industry Training Board
Your Career, 4 — The Designer — leaflet from Clothing and Allied Products Industry Training Board

Film/TV/Radio
BBC Career leaflets — job opportunities in the BBC
Design Appointments
Make-up
Costume
Film Training
All leaflets issued by BBC Appointments, Broadcasting House, London W1A 1AA
Careers in Film and TV — free leaflet from British Film Institute
Careers Special No. 10 *Radio, TV, Theatre and Cinema* — published by COIC
Education and Training for Film and TV — edited by Dennis Boxall. Available from British Kinematograph Sound and TV Society
Film and TV Studies in Higher Education — available from the British Film Institute

Fine Art
Careers with a BA in Fine Art — available from Birmingham Polytechnic Careers Service
Fine Arts Market Place — edited by Cummings, published Bowker 1978
Some Notes for Young Artists on Galleries and Marketing — by Philip Wright, free from Scottish Arts Council
Selling Your Art Work — Yoseloff 1973

Graphic Design/Advertising
Advertising and Public Relations (Choice of Careers Series) — HMSO Careers and Occupational Information Centre
Career Guide to Professional Practice — issued by the Association of Illustrators

Bibliography

Careers in Medical Art and Medical Charting—issued by the Institute of Medical/Biological Illustrators
Creative Handbook—published by Creative Handbook Ltd, 3 Henrietta Street, London WC2
Graphic Design and Illustration (Career Profiles 20)—published by COIC
List of Advertising Agencies—free leaflet from Institute of Practitioners in Advertising
Medical Illustration as a Career—issued by the Medical Artists Association of Great Britain
Notes on the Career and Training of Technical Illustrators—issued by the Institute of Scientific and Technical Communicators
Survival Kit—issued by Association of Illustrators 1980
Careers in Marketing and Allied Professions—by Felicity Taylor Kogan Page 1980
A Career in Marketing, Advertising and Public Relations—edited by Hart and Lamb issued by Marketing Education Foundation
Employment in Publishing—issued by the Publishers' Association
Working in Printing—published by COIC

Interior design
Careers in Interior Design—published by the Society of Industrial Artists and Designers (SIAD)

Museums and Arts Administration
Bibliography for Museum Studies Students—available from the Department of Museum Studies, University of Leicester
Careers in Museums—issued free by the Museums Association
Courses in Arts Administration—free leaflet available from the Arts Council of Great Britain

Photography
150 Careers in Photography—by Brian Hudson, published by Henry Greenwood and Co Ltd
Directory of Photographic Courses—Henry Greenwood and Co Ltd 1981
Photographic Careers—Southey, Argus Books 1978
So You Want To Be A Photographer—Bensusan, Venton 1973
Working in Photography—Anna Ilott and Leila Jeffries, Batsford 1980
An Eye For The Job—a careers film made by the Printing and Publishers Industrial Training Board and distributed by the Central Film Library—with an accompanying book
Photography (Working In Series)—published by the COIC

3 Addresses
Art and Design Education

Clearing Houses for Course Applications
Art and Design Admissions Registry (ADAR)
   24 Widemarsh Street, Hereford HR4 9EP
Clearing House for Postgraduate Courses in Art Education
   The Manor House, Heather, Leicestershire LE6 1QP
Central Teacher Training Registry
   3 Crawford Place, London W1H 2BN
Graduate Teacher Training Registry
   3 Crawford Place, London W1H 2BN
The Universities Central Council on Admissions (UCCA)
   PO Box 28 Cheltenham, Gloucestershire GL50 1HY

Council for National Academic Awards (CNAA)
   344-354 Gray's Inn Road, London WC1X 8BP
Department of Education and Science (DES)
   Elizabeth House, York Road, London SE1 7PH
Technician Education Council (DATEC Courses)
   76 Portland Place, London W1N 4AA
National Union of Students (NUS)
   3 Endsleigh Street, London WC1

Regional Advisory Councils for Further and Higher Education
(each council publishes an annual Directory of all courses in the region)
London and Home Counties Regional Advisory Council for Technological Education
   Tavistock House South, Tavistock Square, London WC1H 9LR.
East Anglian Regional Advisory Council for Further Education
   Shirehall, Bury St Edmunds IP33 2AN
East Midland Further Education Council
   Robins Wood House, Robins Wood Road, Aspley, Nottingham NG8 3NH
Northern Council for Further Education
   5 Grosvenor Villas, Grosvenor Road, Newcastle upon Tyne NE2 2RU
North Western Regional Advisory Council for Further Education
   The Town Hall, Walkden Road, Worsley, Manchester M28 4QE
Southern Regional Council for Further Education
   26 Bath Road, Reading RG1 6NT

Addresses

South West Regional Council for Further Education
   Wessex Lodge, 11/13 Billetfield, Taunton, Somerset TA1 3NN
Welsh Joint Education Committee
   245 Western Avenue, Cardiff CF5 2YX
West Midlands Advisory Council for Further Education
   Norfolk House, Smallbrook Queensway, Birmingham B5 4NB
Yorkshire and Humberside Association for Further and Higher Education
   Bowling Green Terrace, Jack Lane, Leeds LS11 9SX

General Professional Bodies and Organisations

General
Arts Council of Great Britain,
   105 Piccadilly, London W1V 0AU
Arts Council of Northern Ireland
   181a Stranmillis Road, Belfast BT9 5DU
Crafts Council
   12 Waterloo Place, London SW1Y 4AU
Design Council
   The Design Centre, 28 Haymarket, London SW1Y 4SU
Royal Society of Arts
   8 John Adam Street, London WC2
Scottish Arts Council
   19 Charlotte Street, Edinburgh EH2 4DF
Scottish Design Council
   72 St Vincents Street, Glasgow G2
Society of Industrial Artists and Designers (SIAD)
   12 Carlton House Terrace, London SW1Y 5AH
Welsh Arts Council
   Museum Place, Cardiff CF1 3NX
Welsh Design Council
   Pearl Assurance House, Greyfriars Road, Cardiff CF1 3JN

Regional Arts Associations
Eastern Arts Association
   8-9 Bridge Street, Cambridge CB2 1UA
East Midlands Arts Association
   Mountfields House, Forest Road, Loughborough, Leicestershire LE11 3HU
Greater London Arts Association
   25-31 Tavistock Place, London WC1
Lincolnshire and Humberside Arts
   St Hugh's, Newport, Lincoln LN1 3DN

Addresses
Merseyside Arts Association
 Bluecoat Chambers, School Lane, Liverpool L1 3BX
Northern Arts
 10 Osborne Terrace, Newcastle upon Tyne NE2 1NZ
North West Arts
 52 King Street, Manchester M2 4LY
Southern Arts Association
 19 Southgate Street, Winchester SO23 7EB
South East Arts Association
 9-10 Crescent Road, Tunbridge Wells Kent TN2 2LU
South West Arts
 23 Southernhay East, Exeter, Devon EX1 1QL
West Midlands Arts
 Lloyds Bank Chambers, Market Street, Stafford ST16 2AP
Yorkshire Arts Association
 Glyde House, Glydegate, Bradford, Yorks BN5 0BQ
North Wales Association for the Arts
 10 Wellfield House, Bangor, Gwynedd LL57 1ER
South East Wales Arts Association
 Victoria Street, Cwmbfan, Gwent NP4 3JP
West Wales Association for the Arts
 Dark Gate, Red Street, Carmarthen, Dyfed, West Glamorgan

Other useful general addresses
Artlaw Services Ltd
 358 Strand, London WC2
Art Services Grants and Space (SPACE)
 6-8 Rosebery Avenue, London WC2E 9LG
Association of Artists and Designers in Wales
 17 Nant Fawr, Crescent, Cardiff
Association for Business Sponsorship of the Arts
 3 Pierrepoint Place, Bath
British Crafts Centre
 43 Earlham Street, Covent Garden, London WC2H 9LD
Careers Research and Advisory Centre (CRAC)
 Bateman Street, Cambridge CB2 1LZ
Careers and Occupational Information Centre (COIC)
 Manpower Services Commission, Moorfoot, Sheffield S1 4PQ
City and Guilds of London Institute
 76 Portland Place, London W1N 4AA
Council for Small Industries in Rural Areas (CoSIRA)
 Headquarters, 141 Castle Street, Salisbury, Wiltshire
Crafts Council of Ireland Ltd
 Thomas Prior House, Merrion Road, Ballsbridge, Dublin 4

Addresses

Design and Industries Association (DIA)
  12 Carlton House Terrace, London SW1
Department of Industry, (Small Firms Service)
  123 Victoria Street, London SW1E 6RB
Federation of British Craft Societies
  80a Southampton Row, London WC1B 4BA
Institute of Contemporary Arts
  Nash House, 12 Carlton House Terrace, London SW1
Scottish Craft Centre
  Acheson House, Comongate, Edinburgh EH8 8DD
Small Firms Information Centre
  57 Bothwell Street, Glasgow G2 6TU
Small Firms Information Centre
  16 St Davids House, Wood Street, Cardiff CF1 1ER
Society of Designer Craftsmen Limited
  24 Rivington Street, London, EC2
Workshop and Studio Provision Scotland (WASPS)
  Room 323, Central Chambers, 11 Bothwell Street, Glasgow
  G2 6LY and at — 16 Dublin Street, Edinburgh
Welsh Development Agency, Small Business Unit
  6 Ladywell House, Park Street, Newtown, Powys SY16 1JB
Winston Churchill Memorial Trust
  15 Queen's Gate Terrace, London SW7 5PR

Organisations Associated with Specific Professions

ADVERTISING/PUBLISHING
Advertising Association
  Abford House, 15 Wilton Road, London SW1
Communication, Advertising and Marketing Education Foundation Ltd (CAM Foundation)
  Abford House, 15 Wilton Road, London SW1
Institute of Practitioners in Advertising
  44 Belgrave Square, London SW1X 8QS
Publishers' Association
  19 Bedford Square, London WC1 3HJ

ANTIQUES/ART DEALERS
British Antique Dealers Association
  20 Rutland Gate, London SW7 1BD
Christie's, (Christie's Fine Art Course)
  63b Old Brompton Road, London SW7 3JS
Sotheby, Parke, Bernet and Co, (Works of Art Course)
  33-35 New Bond Street, London, W1A 2AA

Addresses

ARTS ADMINISTRATION/COMMUNITY ARTS
Association of Community Artists (London Office)
   Meanwhile Gardens, Elkstone Road, London, W10 5NT
Society of Professional Arts Administrators
   c/o 74 Lavington Road, London W13

ART EDUCATION
National Association for Design Education
   29 Park Crescent, Oadby, Leicestershire LE2 5YJ
National Society for Art Education
   7a High Street, Corsham, Wiltshire, SN13 0ES

ART THERAPY
British Association of Art Therapists
   13c Northwood Road, London N6 5TL

CONSERVATION
Association of British Picture Restorers
   c/o Cooke and Sons Ltd, Station Avenue, Richmond, Surrey TW9 3QA
Crafts Council Conservation Section
   12 Waterloo Place, London SW1Y 4AU
International Institute for Conservation of Historic and Artistic Works
   6 Buckingham Street, London WC2N 6BA
UK Institute for Conservation
   c/o Conservation Department, Tate Gallery, Millbank, London SW1P 4RG

DISPLAY
British Display Society
   24 Ormond Road, Richmond, Surrey TW10 6TH
Distributive Industry Training Board
   Maclaren House, Talbot Road, Stretford, Manchester M32 0FP
Distributive Trades Education and Training Council
   56 Russell Square, London WC1B 4HP
Retail Distributor's Association
   1 Argyll Street, London W1V 2LH

FASHION/TEXTILES
Carpet Industry Training Board
   Evelyn House, 32 Alderley Road, Wilmslow, Cheshire SK9 1NZ
Cotton and Allied Textiles Industry Training Board
   10th Floor, Sunlight House, Quay Street, Manchester M3 3LH

Addresses

Clothing and Allied Products Industry Training Board
  Towers House, Merrion Way, Leeds, LS2 8NY
Clothing Institute
  Hillview Gardens, Hendon, London NW4 2JS
Knitting, Lace and Net Industry Training Board
  4 Hamilton Road, Nottingham, NG5 1AU
Man Made Fibres Producing Industry Training Board
  Langwood House, 63-81 High Street, Rickmansworth, WD3 1EQ
Society of Dyers and Colourists
  Perkin House, PO Box 244, 82 Grattan Road, Bradford, W Yorkshire
Textiles Institute (textiles technology)
  10 Blackfriars Street, Manchester M3 5DR

FINE ART
Association of Print Workshops
  5 Chiserley Hall, Old Town, Hebden Bridge, W Yorkshire HX7 8SD
British Council, Fine Art Department
  97-99 Park Street, London W17 4NJ
Printmakers Council, Clerkenwell Workshops
31 Clerkenwell Close, London EC1

FILM/TV/RADIO
Association of Cinematograph, Television and Allied Technicians
  2 Soho Square, London W1V 6DD
BBC Appointments
  Broadcasting House, London W1A 1AA
British Film Institute
  127 Charing Cross Road, London WC2H 0EA
British Kinematograph, Sound and TV Society, Education and Training Committee
  110-112 Victoria House, Vernon Place, London WC1B 4DJ
Independent Broadcasting Authority
  70 Brompton Road, London SW3 1EY

FURNITURE
British Furniture Manufacturers Federated Associations
  30 Harcourt Street, London W1

GRAPHIC DESIGN/ILLUSTRATION
Association of Illustrators
  17 Carlton House Terrace, London SW1Y 5AH

Addresses
British Printing Industries Federation
   11 Bedford Row, London WC1R 4DX
Institute of Packaging
   1a Elm Park, Stanmore, Middlesex HA7 4BZ
Institute of Scientific and Technical Communicators
   17 Blueridge Avenue, Brockmans Park, Hatfield, Hertfordshire
Medical Artists' Association of Great Britain
   54 Palmer Park Avenue, Reading, Berkshire
Institute of Medical and Biological Illustrators
   27 Craven Street, London WC2N 5NX
Society of Graphic Artists
   17 Carlton House Terrace, London SW1
Society of Typographic Designers, The Honorary Secretary
   1 Rochester Square, London NW1
Printing and Publishing Industry Training Board
   Merit House, Edgware Road, London NW9

INTERIOR DESIGN
Association of Exhibition Organisers
   10 Manchester Square, London W1M 5AH
British Display Society
   24 Ormond Road, Richmond, Surrey
British Institute of Interior Design
   22-24 South Street, Ilkeston, Derbyshire

JEWELLERY/SILVERSMITHING/CERAMICS
Goldsmiths' Company
   Goldsmiths' Hall, Foster Lane, London EC2
The Institute of Ceramics
   Federation House, Stoke-on-Trent ST4 2RT

MUSEUMS
Museums Association
   34 Bloomsbury Way, London WC1A 2SF

PHOTOGRAPHY
Associatiaon of Fashion, Advertising and Editorial Photographers
   10a Dryden Street, Covent Garden, London WC2
Bureau of Freelance Photographers
   Steward House, 59 Tottenham Lane, London N8 9BE
Institute of Incorporated Photographers
   Anwell End, Ware, Hertfordshire SG12 9AN
Master Photographers' Association
   1 West Ruislip Station, Ruislip, Middlesex, HA4 7DW

Addresses

National Council for the Training of Journalists
 Carlton House, Hemnall Street, Epping, Essex CM16 9NL (for press photography)
Royal Photographic Society of Great Britain
 14 South Audley Street, London W1

INDEX

Artists
  definition 12, 16
  earning a living 17
  necessary aptitudes 32, 33

Artlaw 91

Art Schools and Faculties of Art and Design 23
  annual exhibitions, 'open days' 39, 47
  definitions of 23, 46
  evolution of 23
  interviews 37, 39, 40
  polytechnic faculties and colleges of HE 26, 43, 46
  preparing for interview 39, 40
  professional tutors 48
  training and vocational objectives 25, 28
  visits to 39, 45

Arts Council of Great Britain 17, 24
  grants, financial assistance 95

Art Teaching—courses
  entry requirements 79
  craft, design technology 67
  higher and adult education 67
  how and when to apply 79, 80
  routes of training 65, 66

British Broadcasting Corporation
  costume department 128
  film trainee scheme 106
  graphics department 107

British Display Society 61
  national diplomas 62

British Institute of Interior Design 61
  associate membership 62

Careers Research Advisory Centre
  publications 57, 71, 73

City and Guilds of London
  certificates 69
  photography qualification 104

Clothing Institute 62

Council for National Academic Awards
  degree awarding body 55
  degrees 46
  publications 56, 64, 67, 73, 74, 76
  role of 43

College studies
  choice of course and college 44, 45
  competition for entry 27, 28
  entry to the professions 26
  links with industry 48
  need for 25
  professional/recreational studies 41
  qualifications, growing importance 27
  subject specialisation 34
  two-part system, CNAA/DATEC 43, 59

Communication Advertising and Marketing Foundation 61
  creative diploma 62

Crafts Advisory Council 24

Crafts Council 11, 24
  grants to craftsmen 95

Crafts and the craftsman
  abilities needed 32
  artist/designer-craftsmen 20, 92,

Index

94, 109, 110, 111, 130
crafts revival 15, 92, 131
craft traditions 21
definitions 13, 20, 22
designer-craftsmen 14, 15, 20, 22, 92
industrial crafts 109, 110
marketing, outlets for work 29, 92
the production process 21, 92, 110, 112

DATEC courses
age of entry 36, 45, 58
course structure, content 42, 57,
duration, length of study 58
entry requirements 36, 57, 58, 78
foundation studies 53, 59
how and when to apply 79
mode of study, type of course 41, 43, 45, 58, 59
national clearing house 79
national validation 43, 46, 57
Technician Education Council 41
training for design industry 58
transfer to degree courses 45, 57 75, 76

Department of Education and Science
bursaries 83
publication 84
student numbers 86

Design Council 11, 24
designers' register 91
publications 54, 57, 63, 81

Design and Industries Association 24

Design and the Designer
abilities needed 30, 31, 32, 33
assistant designers 115, 117, 119, 122, 129, 133
consultant design 18, 88, 116, 133
definitions 13, 15, 17, 18, 23
design managers (textiles) 130, 132

engineering design 18, 19, 64
freelance design 18, 87, 88, 116, 133
group design practices 20, 90, 91
industrial, product design 13, 17, 22, 23, 89
job market 28
mechanical and electronic engineering design 20
problem solving 13, 32
the design process 18, 20, 46, 115, 117
training 24
working as a team 20, 32, 89, 91, 97, 106, 107, 133

Drawing
ability to draw 30
commitment to 25
conveying information 31
definitions 30, 31
demonstrating your ability 38
fundamental activity for the designer 23

Employment
advertising of jobs 9, 89, 96
artists' agents 91, 92, 99
artist/designer-craftsmen 92
assistant designer 115, 121
college leaver, getting started 84, 85, 86, 89, 90, 91, 115, 116, 123, 132
consultant designer 18, 88, 116, 133
demand for design 10, 18, 19, 88
design studios, drawing offices 87, 89, 104, 105, 115
employing graduates 29, 87
exhibiting 94
freelance work 87, 89, 90, 96, 99, 121
grants to set up workshops 93, 94, 95
group practices 90, 91
industrial designer 13, 17, 22, 23, 89
legal, financial aid 91, 95
marketing, outlets for work 92, 104, 111, 131

157

Index

place to work 93
portfolio of work 85, 86, 90
routine work 90, 97, 102, 132
setting up a workshop or business 93, 94, 95
working at home 18, 87
workshops, collective studios 93

Folder of work—Portfolio
contents of 37, 38
college/course applications 75, 77
demonstrating ability 37
getting a job 85, 86, 90
need for 36, 37, 75

Foundation course
age of entry 36, 54, 75
choosing a specialisation 35, 36, 45, 53, 54
DATEC and foundation studies 53, 59
definition of 34, 53
discovering your special ability 35
discretionary grants for 35, 53
entry requirements 74
how to apply 75
route to degree courses 53, 76

General courses
art history courses 69, 70, 77
combined, multi-disciplinary courses 71, 72, 73, 77
definitions of 41, 42, 43, 44
diploma in higher education (DipHE) 73, 74, 76
entry requirements 77, 78
how and when to apply 78
job opportunities 72
polytechnic and college of HE courses 77
university courses 43, 44
UCCA handbook 64, 78

Grants
applications 81, 82
discretionary for foundation studies 35
during sandwich placement 56
eligibility 81, 82, 83
mandatory/discretionary awards 81
parental contribution 82
post DipHE courses 74
post-graduate work 69
setting up workshops and studios 93, 94, 95

Institute of Civil Engineers 24

Institute of Incorporated Photographers 61
qualifying examination 62, 104

Institute of Mechanical Engineers 24

Mass production 9, 12, 13, 14, 114
and industrial crafts 110
ceramics 112, 113
fabric industry 130
fashion 121
furniture 113
glass 112
shoe industry 124
silverware/jewellery 110, 111

Museums Association
diploma 135, 136

Occupations
advertising agencies 97, 103, 104, 105
advertising, films, TV 107
advertising, publicity design 93, 97, 107
art and design historian 134
art and design teaching 137, 138, 139
art director, role of 97
art editor 98, 99, 104
arts administration 136
art therapy 140, 141
bookbinding 108, 136
carpet design 133
ceramics 109, 112
chinaware 109

Index

community arts 136, 137, 140
craft potters 112
decorative surfaces 133
design agencies 108
design technicians 105, 106, 116
display design 119
draughtsman 100, 116, 131
dress design 121, 124
educational film/TV making 107, 108
educational graphics/visual aids 108
embroidery 124
engineering design 114
exhibition design 118
fashion accessories 126
fashion buyer 128
fashion design 121, 122, 123, 124, 125
fashion illustrator 127
fashion journalism 127
fashion technician 127
film animation 105
film making 106
film/TV set designer 119, 120
fine art 134
furnishing fabrics 130
furniture design 109, 113
general illustration 99
glassware 109, 112
graphic design 96
industrial ceramics 113
industrial crafts 109
industrial designer 114, 115
industrial designer (engineer) 114
interior decorator 118
interior designer 116
jewellery 109
knitwear 130
lace design 131
layout artists 102, 106
lettering, calligraphy 108
lingerie and corsetry 125
local arts centres 140
medical illustration 100
menswear, sportswear design 126
millinery design 121, 124
model making 101, 116, 118

museums 135, 140
museums, gallery curatorship 134, 135
package design 103
painter, printmaker 137
paper conservator 135
paper pattern design 128
photography 104, 105
picture research 136
picture restoration 135
pottery 109
printed textiles 132
product designer 114
scientific illustration 100
shoe design 124
sign design 102
silverware 109, 110
silversmith 110
television graphics 107
technical draughtsman 116
technical illustration 100
textile design 129
theatrical costume design 128
theatre design 119, 120, 128
typography 101, 102, 103, 107
wall paper design 132
woven fabrics 129

Post graduate study
   definitions of 68
   entry requirements 68, 81
   further preparation for work 84
   MA courses, Royal College of Art 68
   part-time study 83

Problem solving 32, 37, 46, 47
   practical study 46
   skills needed 32

Professional trade training
   age of entry for trade training 44, 69
   day or block release 58, 64, 69, 116, 119, 124, 127
   definition of 60
   design apprenticeship (textile technology) 129
   education and training 63

Index

membership of professional bodies 60, 61, 62
professional bodies awarding qualifications 61, 62
technician training 64, 69
trade based training 41, 44, 69, 104

Regional Advisory Councils 54
course lists, publications 63, 69, 80

Rural Industries Board 24

Small workshops 15, 109, 112, 129, 130

Society of Designer Craftsmen 61

Society of Industrial Artists and Designers 24, 61
designers' register 91
diploma membership 62
levels of membership 63
professional advice 91

Specialist degree courses (CNAA)
age of entry 54, 56
art history as a component of 40, 47, 48, 56, 69
art history courses 69, 70, 77
assessments/exhibitions 47, 48
complementary, related studies 40, 47, 56
definitions of 42, 43, 44, 45, 55
direct entry 53, 76
duration of courses 56
engineering design 64
entry requirements 36, 75
fine art courses—description 49
fine art, as a common course element 55
graphic design courses— description 49
how to apply (clearing house) 76
links with industry 48, 55, 56
low drop out rate 54
main areas of study 48, 55, 96
textile/fashion courses— description 50
three dimensional design courses —description 51
sandwich courses 48, 56
validation of 43

Talent 26
abilities needed 30, 32, 33
art and design as a talent industry 25, 85
commitment and initiative 27, 28, 44, 47
identifying your talent 35
market for 29
outlets for 84
showing your ability 37, 38
visual, practical skills 31, 32, 46
when it develops 37

Textile Institute 61
associate examination 62

Vocational diplomas, certificates (non DATEC)
age of entry 45
college awards (diplomas/ certificates) 43, 60
definitions of 42
duration of courses 60
entry requirements 36, 42, 60, 80
part-time courses 69, 104
reorganisation, national validation 41, 43, 59, 60
technician courses 60